Delivering E-learning for Information Services in Higher Education

PAUL CATHERALL

Chandos Publishing

Oxford · England · New Hampshire · USA

Chandos Publishing (Oxford) Limited
Chandos House
5 & 6 Steadys Lane
Stanton Harcourt
Oxford OX29 5RL
UK
Tel: +44 (0) 1865 884447 Fax: +44 (0) 1865 884448
Email: info@chandospublishing.com
www.chandospublishing.com

Chandos Publishing USA
3 Front Street, Suite 331
PO Box 338
Rollinsford, NH 03869
USA
Tel: 603 749 9171 Fax: 603 749 6155
Email: BizBks@aol.com

First published in Great Britain in 2005

ISBN:
1 84334 088 7 (paperback)
1 84334 095 X (hardback)

© P. Catherall, 2005

British Library Cataloguing-in-Publication Data.
A catalogue record for this book is available from the British Library.

The Publishers make no representation, express or implied, with regard to the accuracy of the information contained in this publication and cannot accept any legal responsibility or liability for any errors or omissions.

The material contained in this publication constitutes general guidelines only and does not represent to be advice on any particular matter. No reader or purchaser should act on the basis of material contained in this publication without first taking professional advice appropriate to their particular circumstances.

Cover images courtesy of Bytec Solutions Ltd (*www.bytecweb.com*) and David Hibberd (*DAHibberd@aol.com*).

Printed and Bound by 4Edge Limited *(www.4edge.co.uk)*

Contents

Preface

As is the case with many emerging technologies, it is often difficult to grasp the significance of new concepts in computer technology amid the hype of buzzwords and jargon. The terms 'e-learning' and 'VLE' have become familiar to many library and information professionals, but what do these terms really mean?

It is hoped that this text will describe, in plain language, the essential features and support issues of systems designed to support teaching and learning via the new medium of communication, the Internet and World Wide Web.

Note on acronyms and technical terms

Acronyms, technical expressions and other uncommon terms are explained in the glossary at the back of the book.

Important note concerning URLs (web addresses) in this book

Throughout this book you will see URLs, e.g. *http://www.w3.org* (web addresses). If you see a URL at the end of a sentence ending in a full stop, ignore the full stop at the end when entering the URL in your web browser; for example, the following address without a stop at the end is correct:

http://www.w3.org

the following address with a stop at the end is incorrect:

http://www.w3.org.

So do not type the full stop at the end of URLs – the only reason it is shown in this book is for punctuation.

Acknowledgements

I Mam, Dad a'r Teulu

I would like to thank the following for their many suggestions and contributions:

Andrea Lawry: Open Text Corporation. Advisor, Ch. 2, FirstClass review.

Anita Pincas: Institute of Education, University of London. Advisor, Ch. 2, FirstClass review.

Anthony Doyle: Middlesbrough College. Advisor, Ch. 6, Middlesbrough NLN Gateway.

Dan Stowell: University College, London. Contributor, Ch. 2, Moodle review.

David Crook: The Copyright Licensing Agency (CLA). Advisor, Ch. 5, Copyright.

Jak Radice: University of Bradford. Contributor, Ch. 2, VLE Case History.

James Everett: Stevenson College, Edinburgh. Advisor, Ch. 2, Teknical review.

Julie Voce: University College, London. Advisor, Ch. 2, WebCT review.

Leanne Grice: Serco Learning. Support for Teknical Virtual Campus VLE.

Dr Liz Falconer: University of the West of England, Bristol. Contributor, Ch. 2, VLE Case History.

Dr Malcolm Murray: University of Durham. Contributor, Ch. 2, VLE Case History.

Merv Stapleton: City of Sunderland College. Advisor, Ch. 2, Blackboard review.

Nick Meara: Aston University, Birmingham. Advisor, Ch. 2, FirstClass review.

Paul Burt/Vicki Simpson: University of Surrey. Contributors, Ch. 2, VLE Case History.

Paul Davis: University of Oxford. Advisor, Ch. 2, Bodington review.

Dr R. A. Stanier: University of Brighton. Contributor, Ch. 2, VLE Case History.

Richard Everett: Oaklands College, Hertfordshire. Advisor, Ch. 2, General comments.

Susan Armitage: Lancaster University. Contributor, Ch. 2, VLE Case History.

Dr Susannah Quinse: City University, London. Contributor, Ch. 2, VLE Case History.

Wayne Owens: Net-Work Internet Ltd. Advisor, Ch. 8, Mobile Technologies.

About the author

Paul Catherall is a qualified information professional based at the North East Wales Institute of Higher Education, where he played a key role in implementing online learning. He is a chartered member of the Chartered Institute of Library and Information Professionals (CILIP) and an associate of the Institute of Learning and Teaching (ILT). Previous research included an AHRB-funded Masters project: 'Resource Description and Control on the World Wide Web'. Paul has also taught information technology with a further education provider.

The author may be contacted at:

E-mail: *elearning@draigweb.co.uk*
Website: *http://elearning.draigweb.co.uk*

Introduction to e-learning

What is e-learning?

Literally speaking, the term e-learning is a contraction of electronic learning, and we may assume this describes an electronic or, more precisely, a computer-based form of learning experience. However, on deeper consideration, we may be forgiven if we cannot readily provide a simple definition for e-learning, a term which has been used heavily in recent years within a wide range of educational contexts.

A typical example of how e-learning is understood is illustrated in a recent article by the Learning and Teaching Support Network (Erskine, 2003):

> E-learning covers a wide set of applications, such as Web-based learning environments, computer-based learning ... and videotape, satellite broadcast, interactive TV and CD-ROM. (p. 3)

In the above example, several forms of technology are cited as examples of e-learning, including traditional electronic media such as video and more recent media such as the Internet.

Although they may seem dissimilar, these technologies share several basic characteristics – they all provide a capacity to publish or present resources, either in the form of video, text or sound, enabling interaction of some form between resource authors and recipients. Educational organisations have long used a range of conventional technologies to support learning and teaching; since the 1970s, the Open University has used audio tapes, video and television to provide lectures for part-time study and distance learning.

In this context, e-learning could be defined as any technology allowing for the delivery of learning resources or communication between tutor and student; this wider view of e-learning, reflecting the uses of audio, visual and other media, is discussed later in this book.

However, one technology in particular has become the predominant medium for e-learning in recent years, this is the Internet and World Wide Web, a literally world-wide communication system, allowing for unprecedented interaction between educators and learners.

It is quickly apparent from a few minutes using an Internet search engine, such as Google, that the majority of references to e-learning discuss a computer medium and an online context, i.e. a learning experience based on the medium of the Internet or the World Wide Web. The rapid rise of e-learning software has been as sudden and as dramatic as the rise of the Internet itself.

Most e-learning technology is web-based and delivered via a web browser, such as Internet Explorer or Netscape Navigator. For users already familiar with web-based applications, this presents an existing skills advantage.

The communication benefits of the Internet and World Wide Web are reflected within many e-learning systems, including the capability to send e-mail, the ability to hyperlink between resources and the ability to publish common document formats, such as Microsoft Word and Excel and Adobe Acrobat. E-learning systems also allow access to resources from any Internet-connected computer, rather than limited access on a university campus.

At this point, we can say that the term e-learning is more popularly used to describe a computer-based and online approach to learning and teaching.

Although it is true to say that e-learning could be defined in terms of the technology upon which it relies, educationalists often emphasise the particular techniques or form of learning associated with education in an electronic context. Good (2001) defines e-learning as a new form of ped-agogy, suggesting that educationalists should demonstrate 'technological fearlessness', and explore new ways of using e-learning within teaching:

> E-learning is different from traditional forms, and demands new pedagogical skills ... keeping an eye out for new technological developments and for new ways of using the technology, autonomously solving problems and learning. (p. 169)

E-learning is therefore also considered as a pedagogical approach, a method of teaching requiring particular teaching methods suitable for an online or digital context.

Although this book is primarily concerned with the operational issue of providing e-learning as a service or facility within information services, it is also important to consider the aims of educationalists in the context of system functionality. Where relevant, this text will suggest practical uses for e-learning features within the context of educational delivery.

In summary, we can conclude that e-learning is not easily defined, but comprises a number of perspectives and interpretations, which may be grouped as follows:

1. e-learning as a basic concept of educational delivery or interaction via technology;

2. e-learning as a particularly computer-based and online method of educational delivery;

3. e-learning as an educational technique (pedagogy).

This text will consider e-learning principally from perspective 2, in accordance with the stated aims of this text, i.e. to describe and comment on a range of e-learning software and implementation issues, although the remaining perspectives may also arise in this context.

Background to e-learning

It could be argued that e-learning is not a new concept; education and research have long provided the impetus for the development of innovative communications technology and, in doing so, laid down the foundations and standards that would become the modern Internet and World Wide Web.

Developed following decades of research, the first network to resemble the Internet of today was launched in 1969 by the US Advanced Research Project Agency (ARPA). This early network, or ARPANET, had been built with the specific aim of creating a distributed communications system capable of sustaining a nuclear attack.

However, agency researchers and scientists quickly realised the wider significance of their invention and before long the ARPANET was being used by its own inventors for a range of academic purposes, including communication via e-mail (developed in 1970) and simple resource sharing (e.g. via file transfer protocol FTP).

By 1983, ARPANET had been superseded by a civilian network mainly run by US universities; this period saw a dramatic growth in connections by universities across the US and Europe.

In 1984, the Joint Academic Network (JANET) was established to regulate Internet use across the UK academic community, with similar organisations emerging in the US (e.g. BITNET, CREN).

Initially restricted to universities and related organisations, the early Internet operated on a non-commercial basis; additionally, access was restricted only to those able to use the relatively complex UNIX-based computer terminals of the time.

However, by the early 1980s new types of computer systems such as IBM's Personal Computer were available, requiring less technical knowledge to operate than earlier systems; this trend, and the emergence of the Microsoft Windows and Apple Macintosh operating systems using a simple mouse-driven interface saw an increase in Internet users at home and in the workplace.

To appreciate the development of electronic learning systems, it may be worth introducing a few fundamental technologies that characterised educational activity on the early Internet. Many of these technologies are still widely in use today.

- *E-mail.* By 1973 three-quarters of Internet traffic was electronic mail (Naughton, 1999), a demonstration of how researchers and academics realised the potential of the Internet as a medium for scholarly exchange. Almost unchanged since its invention in the early 1970s, e-mail contains fields allowing for the effective relay of messages, including Sender, Recipient and Subject. Whereas early e-mail was available only via text-based programs such as PINE, modern e-mail is now accessed using a wide range of graphical, mouse-driven systems and may also be accessed via the World Wide Web.

- *BBS.* Bulletin Board Systems used simple text-based menus to provide discussion forums on a wide range of technical, educational and other subjects. Although the term 'BBS' is still seen on the Internet today, most modern discussion forums use the technology of the World Wide Web.

- *Newsgroups.* An e-mail-based discussion and bulletin service, allowing for posting and display of messages based on subject headings, e.g. 'sci.geology'. Newsgroups (also called Usenet) are still widely used on the Internet, accessed via newsreader software (e.g. Agent: *http://www.forteinc.com/agent/*). Newsgroups may also be accessed directly via web-based services such as Google Usenet (*http://groups.google.com*).

- *Gopher and Veronica.* An early form of document publishing system using a menu interface to select and view files. Gopher allowed for linking to resources on other Gopher servers on the Internet. The Veronica service also provided a facility to search Gopher sites worldwide. Gopher has largely vanished from the modern Internet, superseded by the World Wide Web.

- *FTP and Archie.* FTP is a simple method for sending and receiving files across the Internet; many organisations still use FTP either for internal use or public access. FTP can be used in a variety of ways; one of the easiest is to use an FTP program such as Winsock FTP (*http://www.ipswitch.com*) to connect to FTP servers. FTP remains a popular method of file publishing on the Internet. Archie servers provide a method to search public FTP sites worldwide, traditionally using a command line telnet connection, but web versions are also available (e.g. *http://www.filewatcher.com*).

- *Telnet.* A simple text-based program used to interact with online services, such as a library Online Public Access Catalogue (OPAC). The user must typically type commands or hit keys to perform operations, such as searching for library records. Telnet is now less used as a user interface, having been replaced by graphical and mouse-operated systems.

Perhaps the story of electronic learning really begins with the World Wide Web, or WWW, conceived and invented by Tim Berners-Lee between approximately 1989 and 1993.

Berners-Lee had been employed on several occasions as a systems developer at CERN (the European Laboratory for Particle Physics) in Geneva, with responsibility for developing an electronic information system.

Naughton (1999) describes Berners-Lee's proposal to provide access to information from a range of facility locations, to allow users to update documents themselves and to allow for easy linking between documents:

> The paper concludes with a recommendation that CERN should 'work toward a universal linked information system in which generality and portability are more important than fancy graphics techniques and complex extra facilities.' (p. 235)

The basis of Berners-Lee's system was his 'web browser', an application which ran on any networked computer and displayed Web pages containing all kinds of information on the CERN network.

Importantly, the web browser used a number of existing network standards, an important aspect that would eventually allow this system to be used across the entire Internet.

The web pages displayed by the web browser were simple text files, but also contained a number of tags, which could tell the web browser exactly how to display an individual document. For example, to display a paragraph with spaces above and below the text, part of the file may have looked like this:

> <P>This document is about the development of the World Wide Web</P>

Other tags instructed the web browser to display text in a variety of ways or indicate other descriptive information; for example, the following TITLE tag could be used to indicate the title of a document:

> <TITLE>The History of E-learning</TITLE>

In this way, documents could be customised for display; this type of marked-up text was dubbed hyper-text mark-up language or HTML, and drew inspiration from an earlier format used in the publishing industry (SGML or standard generalized mark-up language.)

Another feature included in HTML by Beners-Lee was the ability to link between documents. Previous systems such as Gopher had relied on structured menus, but Berners-Lee had developed an alternative method of linking based on links from words or phrases in the actual text. Berners-Lee described the electronic document containing links as hypertext and the links themselves as hyperlinks (terms invented by Theodor Nelson, a pioneer of early Internet document systems).

The hyperlink tag consists of an address (the name of the target document to be displayed) and a label (the link that must be followed to view the document), e.g.

> <A HREF="report.htm">The Report</A>

Another feature of this 'web' system was the ability of users to update and author their own web pages, provided they had an understanding of the tags required to 'mark-up' their documents.

Other supporting technology emerged with this early web system, most notably the address format for web documents; this became the

URL (universal resource locator), a common feature of today's web browser, e.g.:

http://www.somewhere.com

Tim Berners-Lee's web browser rapidly spread across the Internet community. Whereas the original web browser required more complex UNIX-based computer systems to operate, newer versions began to appear for use on the increasingly popular IBM PC format. One of the earliest and most popular of these web browsers was Mosaic, developed by Marc Andreessen in 1993. Controversially, this was the first web browser to allow for displaying images in web pages, using a new image tag, e.g. <IMG SRC="myimage.gif">.

In 1990, Berners-Lee dubbed this phenomenon the World Wide Web and by 1995 it had almost overtaken all other forms of activity on the Internet. Naughton (1999) comments·

> ... in two years the volume of Internet traffic involving web pages went from almost nothing to nearly a quarter of the total. (p. 248)

Educational and research organisations quickly took advantage of the Web as a means of easily publishing documents online. The Web did not just allow for basic document delivery, but also allowed for publishing a range of file formats represented by the growing range of word processing, database and other applications available.

The Web also allowed for the creation of portals or gateways dealing with specific themes or subjects that could provide hyperlinks to external web resources.

During the initial expansion of the web, educators and researchers were required to mark-up their HTML documents (web pages) by hand, requiring a knowledge of HTML; the only real alternative was to rely on the expertise of technical staff able to mark up their documents for them.

However, software vendors quickly seized on the idea of the word processor concept, which would allow ordinary users to create documents in HTML format without the need for editing HTML code. Early HTML editors included FrontPage Express on the Microsoft Windows operating system, and Netscape Composer, which came as an integral part of the Netscape web browser.

Like the early Internet, the quickly expanding World Wide Web was still restricted to universities, research centres and similar organisations. However, with decreasing costs and increasingly usable computing, typified by the Microsoft Windows operating system, the World Wide Web steadily expanded among home users.

The growth of home access to the World Wide Web stimulated a continuing commercial trend in Internet usage, but also opened up new opportunities for remote access to educational resources by students and staff.

Advanced web technologies have since emerged to support conventional HTML documents (e.g. Java, Javascript, ASP), with web browsers now able to allow increased interaction by the user. Educators and students are able to communicate by sharing files, or chat in real-time by typing messages which are displayed instantly on the page for all participants to see.

It is in the context of this modern web technology that e-learning systems have recently expanded and become one of the most prolific aspects of the World Wide Web.

It is important to remember that web-based learning systems are inherently founded upon the Internet technology that went before. The development of e-learning is really the story of how Internet concepts, from early bulletin board systems and e-mail, have been combined and refined to provide today's technology.

One of the most useful things to remind any student who may be familiar with a web browser but is confused by web-based learning is the simple fact that (from the user's perspective) 'it's really just a web page'.

HE environment

In considering the current context of e-learning within higher education (HE), it may perhaps be useful to consider a few wider developments in the HE sector.

Since the mid-1990s there has been significant emphasis from UK governments for the widening of access to education by the British public, primarily as a force for improving the skills of Britain's workforce.

Coffield and Williamson (1997) suggest that the rise of new information-based industries and decline of traditional industrial activity has brought new demands on governments to nurture workforce skills:

> Throughout Europe ... governments are keen to strengthen core skills – numeracy, communication, information technology and

interpersonal effectiveness – and the vocational relevance of study programmes. (p. 8)

Government-funded bodies and professional organisations have published a number of influential reports on the issue of widening educational participation, portraying educational activity as a necessarily lifelong process or 'lifelong learning', central to the well-being both of the learner and the nation as a whole.

Perhaps the decisive event in the debate on changing skill demands within the UK came with the publication of the *Dearing Report* (1997) by the National Committee of Inquiry into Higher Education, which discussed the need for increased university participation, but also suggested the use of new technology to widen the range of approaches to deliver teaching and learning:

New technology is changing the way information is stored and transmitted ...

It opens up the possibility of Higher Education programmes being offered remotely by anyone anywhere in the world, in competition with existing UK institutions, but also offers a global market place ... (paragraph 20)

Other reports have highlighted the need for wider participation among individuals whose background fell outside the traditional profile of university entrants; the government green paper *The Learning Age* (1998) highlighted the need for flexible schemes to enable access to HE at an induction level.

A range of regional schemes have emerged to provide access to HE within local communities, often providing opportunities that bridge the gap between further and higher education, such as the Community University of North Wales (*http://www.cunw.ac.uk*).

In addition to widening university access, another recent government aim comprises the reformation or realignment of traditional universities to provide the kind of courses and skills required by modern industry.

The government report *21st Century Skills: Realising our Potential* (2003) discusses the advantages of delivering a 'demand-based' HE system, as opposed to a 'supply-based' system, which itself dictates the nature of education available; in effect, this advocates for a controversial shift in emphasis from traditional academic subjects to vocation-based courses:

There are four principles underlying our approach to improved publicly-funded training provision for adults. It should:

- Be led by the needs of employers and learners.

- Be shaped by the skill needs prioritised in each sector, region and locality.

- Make the best use of Information and Communications Technology (ICT) to deliver and assess learning.

- Give colleges and training providers maximum discretion to decide how best to respond to needs ... (p. 87)

Most recently, the government's White Paper *The Future of Higher Education* (2003) outlines radical proposals to reform the HE sector, including 'support (for) those from disadvantaged backgrounds by restoring grants, helping with fee costs, and abolishing up-front tuition fees ...' (p. 6). The paper also proposes an additional student 'contribution' up to £3,000 to supplement existing course fees; this is intended to finance bursaries for less financially able students (among universities implementing the 'top-up' fee).

But how does widening participation or 'lifelong learning' relate to e-learning?

E-learning and related systems used to support learning and teaching are quickly becoming an important feature of the rapidly changing climate in HE provision.

Several radical changes have occurred in HE over recent years, partly as a result of government advocacy, and partly as a direct response to social and economic trends. Primarily there has been a steady increase in university uptake in recent years, with an increase of 4.3 per cent between 2001 and 2003 (Office of National Statistics, 2003d).

One of the most startling features of the new university landscape is the significant shift from entrants of a predominantly 17–18-year-old age range to a much wider range. In 2000, there were 77,400 full-time, first-year HE students over the age of 25, but by 2001 this figure had reached almost 83,000, an increase of 7 per cent.

Another emerging trend can be seen in the rising number of part-time applicants, with an increase of 3 per cent from 2000 to 2002:

1,236,300 (66%) of all enrolments are full-time, an increase in numbers of 3% since 2000/01. The number of part-time enrolments also grew by 3% over the same period. (Office of National Statistics, 2003c)

These statistics reflect both emerging barriers to HE and changing study patterns.

With the gradual introduction of university fees during the 1990s and depreciation of the maintenance grant, the choice of going to university is now a financial decision as much as an educational one, prompting many to consider the longer-term approach of delaying education until later life or of part-time study, whilst also working.

The impetus for widening participation and resulting diversity in university entrants has increased demand for support services able to facilitate the requirements of this on-traditional client base. A recent article in the *CILIP Update Journal* (April 2004) comments:

> As Higher Education attempts to diversify its income base in response to uncertain funding futures, the educational landscape is changing. It will be common for all students to do at least part of their studying off site. Increasingly, corporate customers will need learning delivered in situ and will expect to find the resources and skills materials accessible on demand ... (p. 24)

Additionally, the Disability Discrimination Act 1995 and more recent Special Educational Needs and Disability Act 2001 both outline requirements for the provision of HE for users with disabilities. A report by City University, London (2003) indicates that 4.6 per cent of HE students have a disability, with numbers expected to rise in the future (see Chapter 5).

The typical scenario born of these trends could be summarised as follows:

■ growth in demand for technical, business-related and other vocational subjects;

■ growth of the part-time student base;

■ growth in the numbers of non-traditional students (including mature students) requiring support for development of core study skills;

■ increasing legal remit to support students possessing disabilities, including visual and other access requirements;

- increase in low-contact study, requiring flexible approaches to learning, teaching and communication.

It is in the context of these market-led forces and emphases for widening access that the Internet and e-learning has recently emerged as an innovative means for supporting the delivery of HE.

The following pages demonstrate how e-learning systems may be used to fulfil the particular demands of this changing HE climate.

Approaches to e-learning

A diverse range of sophisticated software designed to facilitate learning and teaching has emerged since the mid 1990s. With the obvious advent of the Internet and World Wide Web, many of these tools are web-based and rely on the Internet for user access. The use of the web browser to access the e-learning system presents obvious advantages, because many users may have used the Web at some stage, either at home, in education or at public libraries.

Perhaps the single most important characteristic of e-learning lies in the attempt by many systems to provide an interface that is both intuitive and usable. Typically, the user is presented with a screen, which allows for interaction and user-input using the familiar mouse, often displaying options, buttons and other controls similar to those found in the familiar Microsoft Windows operating system.

In former years, users were often challenged to upload and manage their own documents on the early Internet and World Wide Web. A common scenario might have been something like this.

1. A chemistry lecturer in HE wishes to publish his or her course timetable (a Microsoft Word document) on the department website; the website may be updated by department staff, but he lacks the technical skills to update the web page himself.

2. Our lecturer passes his timetable to another chemist, the web champion for this department, who has the basic skills to update the web page.

3. The web champion copies the timetable document to an appropriate location on the web server, then edits the departmental web page using the FrontPage application, adding a hyperlink to the correct location or path of the timetable.

4. Users are now able to access the timetable from the new link on the department website.

Compare the above with the following scenario, describing the same task, but using a web-based e-learning system.

1. A chemistry lecturer in HE wishes to publish his course timetable (a Microsoft Word document) on the department e-learning area; he logs into his computer and clicks on the Internet Explorer icon on his desktop (his web browser). The institute homepage is displayed.

2. Our lecturer follows a link from the institute homepage to the e-learning system. The e-learning login page is displayed, and he logs in using his normal university details.

3. Once logged in, the lecturer selects the specific online course he wishes to update, then clicks on the 'administration' area to upload his file.

4. Users are now able to access the timetable via the appropriate online course within the e-learning system.

The above comparison typifies the kind of control educators and other staff may exercise via e-learning systems, both in managing online content and interacting with their user base.

Similar comparisons may be made between traditional and recent approaches to the student experience in accessing web-based resources and interacting with tutors. The traditional website consisted of fairly static pages, i.e. they displayed textual or graphical content, or linked to other similar pages, but presented minimal scope for interaction between student, system and tutor. However, e-learning systems often allow for a wide range of activities via the web interface, incorporating many Internet features such as e-mail and discussion forums. Consider the following comparison of traditional web-based publishing and recent e-learning systems.

Traditional web publishing

- *Static content.* Pages could be changed by the author but were not dynamic, i.e. web content could not easily be configured to display events in today's diary or provide a personalised view for individual users (e.g. custom layout).

- *Updates to pages required technical knowledge.* Although web editing software such as FrontPage provided a 'word processor' feel for authoring web pages, a knowledge of basic Internet tools and HTML was still often required, limiting the possibility for immediate authorship and control over web content to technical staff and enthusiasts.

- *Limited communication between content authors and viewers.* Any form of interaction by the viewer, e.g. via a web feedback form or discussion forums, was previously impossible without a basic knowledge of complex web technologies such as CGI (common gateway interface) or ASP (active server pages).

- *Limited security.* Restricting access to non-users was difficult without custom-designed systems or reliance on often basic password authentication.

E-learning systems

- *Dynamic web content.* Allowing for custom pages and personalised information based on a user login.
- *Pages easily updated by non-technical users.*
- *Allows for a range of communication tools.* For example, e-mail, discussion forums, real-time chat, file exchange and group tools for collaboration between students.
- *Advanced security features.* Allowing for single sign-on to access a number of systems using only one login.

E-learning systems often function according to particular approaches or concepts, loosely associated with formal approaches to teaching. Some e-learning systems rely heavily on communication features, whereas others provide more scope for the publication of documents and other digital resources.

Let us consider a few common activities or approaches among e-learning systems:

- *Collaboration.* Collaboration tools often involve the exchange of information, documents or other files by users. The Colloquia system is a good example of a collaboration system, in which e-mail is used to discuss topics and share files. In other systems, collaboration may involve shared access to the same file or document. The emphasis of collaboration is often not simply the exchange of material, but a shared process for development of a finished product.

- *Document management and publishing.* This is a feature seen in most e-learning systems, allowing non-technical users to upload (add) documents and other resources to a web-based location. Documents are often arranged or managed using a hierarchy or folder structure. For example, clicking on a folder called 'Course Notes' could result in the current view changing to display the contents of the new folder. Document management features may be used within e-learning systems to provide a simple document repository for students, or may be used more dynamically to provide relevant resources at particular times during a course. Many e-learning systems also allow for document searching within particular online courses and provision for metadata, to describe documents for effective indexing and retrieval. The process of document publishing on the e-learning system should not be confused with the content management system model, comprising a system allowing for online document publishing in a generic context.

- *Synchronous communication.* A real-time form of communication in which individuals may exchange textual messages or other resources within the same time frame. For example, a lecturer could invite students to log into an e-learning system at a specific time to access a chat tool; students and staff could then type comments and view each other's messages on-screen. The disadvantage of synchronous communication is its obvious transience, because chat-based events are often difficult to record; however, this form of communication is invaluable for distance learning and low-contact teaching, where debate can take place online in lieu of the real classroom.

- *Asynchronous communication.* As opposed to synchronous communication, this form of exchange is carried out over an indefinite time scale. The 'discussion board' or 'forum' is an example of this kind of communication tool, in which messages and responses may be typed in the context of a particular topic or subject. For example, a tutor could invite students to debate a topic on an e-learning discussion forum. Students could add their messages at their own convenience; messages would remain on the system for users to review and respond to at any time.

- *Course-work submission.* A range of tools are provided by e-learning systems to allow for document submission to tutors. The traditional method of sending documents as an e-mail attachment to the e-mail address of specified tutors is one basic approach. On Blackboard and other e-learning systems, the 'digital drop-box' feature allows students to upload a document directly via the web page, which is then made available for staff in the administration area.

- *Distance learning.* This term broadly describes any course of study entailing reduced contact time between tutors and students; more correctly, however, distance learning is used to describe courses taught entirely, or almost entirely, via forms of long-distance communication. E-learning systems provide a range of communication features useful for distance-based and low-contact learning, including real-time chat, discussion forums and file submission.

- *Blended learning (or distributed learning).* This term describes the use of a range of approaches to learning within an educational context; in the case of e-learning, blended learning typically indicates the use of electronic systems alongside traditional forms of class-based teaching.

- *Ubiquitous learning.* This term is often used to describe the relationship between students, tutors and electronic systems in a variety of contexts such as the university, home, workplace, local library or via mobile devices such as an Internet-enabled mobile phone (see Chapter 8, Mobile learning). The growth in low-contact teaching has resulted in an increasing dependence on e-learning systems, raising a number of challenges to support a ubiquitous approach to study and communication.

It is important to consider that e-learning systems merely provide tools to facilitate teaching and learning; the practice of e-learning often succeeds when systems are used in an exploratory or inventive fashion by educators, rather than in a prescribed manner. Similarly, the value of consultation with academic and related staff should not be underestimated in selecting, designing or deploying e-learning systems. Consider this comment from Jolliffe et al. (2001):

> The World Wide Web has great potential for use in the delivery of learning to a variety of people. However, as with many learning delivery tools, those involved in the design and development of the materials being delivered and the set up of the actual tool itself find themselves overindulging in the use of the many resources available to them in a Web environment and ignoring the basic principles of learning. (p. 3)

Resource issues

A number of material issues should be considered before selecting, obtaining and deploying an e-learning system. Central issues to consider include staffing, finance, computer hardware and the wider network or systems infrastructure within the host institution.

Staffing an e-learning system should be considered within a range of functions, some of which may overlap across individual staff.

First, there are requirements for technical expertise to prepare and possibly build a server computer capable of running the e-learning software; staff will also be required to install and configure the software on the server, possibly assisted by consultancy from an e-learning company or a related organisation. External consultancy is an added cost that may be required depending on in-house expertise.

Staff will also be required to provide high-level administration on the system, configuring the general appearance of the user interface to match institutional preferences and perform daily administrative functions, such as user accounts management.

Provision should also be made for academic liaison to coordinate system activity with academic departments and provide training for institute staff and students; this role will necessitate the authoring of support manuals for students and staff, including hardcopy and online resources.

Additionally, provision should be made for user support at the front-end of service delivery, possibly via enquiry desk staff within an information services area.

The second resource issue comprises finance, including the costs of staffing, software purchase or licensing (i.e. a fixed-term purchase which is renewed or re-purchased following expiry), and purchase of any computer equipment required.

Hardware requirements for the purchase of a server to provide an e-learning system (as a network service) are usually based on the projected number of users requiring access to the system; guidance for hardware purchasing is normally provided by the software company, including any recommended computer models, hard-drive capacity, memory capacity or other requirements, such as an industry standard database system (e.g. SQL, ORACLE).

Not all e-learning software is distributed commercially, and some of the most popular, such as the Bodington or Moodle systems, are distributed on a not-for-profit or open-source basis.

Care should be taken when considering the benefits of commercial as opposed to open-source e-learning solutions, with some not-for-profit systems lacking in support provision; additionally, there may be extra support costs (i.e. not covered by the basic cost of the software).

Another issue to consider in obtaining support for system maintenance is the support location, with some overseas vendors providing only limited support outside their country of origin.

Existing resources and systems within the institution may also determine whether particular systems are viable. Some e-learning systems may require a range of supporting network services, such as firewalls (to monitor or limit system access), or a compatible student records system, such as SITS.

Further details on resources required for specific e-learning systems are provided in Chapter 2.

Challenges in e-learning

The delivery of learning and teaching via e-learning systems is an issue that attracts both controversy and debate. In the current climate of HE, with rising levels of part-time and mature student uptake, new challenges are rapidly becoming apparent at the practitioner level. And despite technical innovation, e-learning systems remain bound by the physical constraints of the current Internet.

Although high-speed Internet access is steadily gaining popularity (broadband), the delivery of high-bandwidth content such as digital video is still problematic for home Internet users. To ensure widespread availability, care should be taken to minimise the file size of web-published resources. For example, if we published a PowerPoint presentation online of 5 megabytes this could take an hour or longer to download from a home Internet connection using a modem. For more information on reducing file size, see Chapter 3 (Publishing on the VLE).

Additionally, it should not be assumed that all students will be able to access an e-learning system outside the place of study; currently, 48 per cent of UK households have Internet access, with approximately 25 per cent using fast broadband access and the remaining 75 per cent using a slower modem connection (E-Government and Public Sector IT News, 2004). Strategies for supporting users without home Internet access may include providing extended opening hours for institutional IT labs, provision of institute computers/laptops with an Internet service provider package to connect online, or even standard availability of study resources in hardcopy format.

Another challenge in facilitating the delivery of e-learning is the training needs of users, including educators, students and other institutional staff.

The current trend for widening access, encompassing a range of university induction schemes and industrial co-operation, has brought an influx of non-traditional university entrants, some of whom may lack core study skills or information technology (IT) skills expected of sixth-form or FE applicants.

Widening access and an older user base have also brought an increased intake of students possessing disabilities and access difficulties (for discussion on access issues, see Chapter 5).

Teaching staff will require training and support to perform e-learning system functions; perhaps the key prerequisite for successfully delivering an e-learning system lies in instilling support for e-learning among educational practitioners.

Barriers to involvement by educational staff may include lack of confidence in personal IT skills, apprehension at the prospect of radical changes to working practices or concern for the student response to e-learning.

Approaches to address these concerns may include:

- reassurance for staff that systems simply provide an additional resource or tool intended to support existing teaching practices;

- emphasis for staff that they should lead the way systems are used;

- demonstration of key system tools and features, illustrating possible benefits for document publishing, student communication, document submission and other practical features;

- development of department strategies to develop the use of e-learning in consultation with staff;

- reinforce IT skills for staff by providing core skills workshops such as ECDL (the European Computer Driving Licence).

The support issues in implementing an e-learning system for students are similar – students may feel isolated if there is a perceived over-reliance on communication via e-learning systems; additionally, students may also lack self-directed study skills important for low-contact study. Methods to support student activity in e-learning may include:

- *Establish usable support systems.* A variety of support methods should be in place to ensure users may obtain help for either technical or course-related enquiries. Use of web feedback forms, support booklets and trained front-end staff can all support user needs.

- *Ensure system usability.* Systems should be researched, tested and piloted to ensure they can be used easily and effectively; a confusing system may create barriers to course participation.

- *Accessibility provision.* Systems should be researched to ensure they meet international accessibility standards such as WCAG (web content accessibility guidelines); users with disabilities may require liaison with qualified disability support staff or access to assistive technology (e.g. screen readers).

- *Induction process.* An effective induction process, in collaboration with tutors and other induction events, should be used to introduce the e-learning system at an early stage in system use.

- *Printing and document distribution.* As resources delivered via e-learning are digital, care should be taken not to 'unload' printing costs onto students; agreement should be reached to ensure critical or otherwise appropriate documentation is available in hardcopy format (e.g. student handbook, coursework submission forms, revision notes).

Other related challenges may involve support for overseas students undertaking distance learning, or support for tutors who may also be based remotely.

Challenges in the context of e-learning also include the need for awareness of current issues, including the e-learning systems market, technical and industry standards and HE sector issues such as accessibility, data protection, copyright and other legal aspects. Subsequent chapters will explore these issues in greater depth.

2

Virtual learning environments

Definition of a VLE

So far, we have considered e-learning in the context of communication, collaboration and other educational activities undertaken in an online environment. Whereas e-learning may be considered as a global or general concept in defining online educational systems or approaches, another key phrase has recently emerged to define a particular model or framework for e-learning systems. The VLE or virtual learning environment is a phrase used to define systems comprising a range of e-learning characteristics and features.

But couldn't we say that all e-learning systems are VLEs? Some e-learning tools provide a particular approach to content delivery or communication; for example, the Colloquia system is based entirely on collaboration via e-mail technology. However, the VLE typically provides a range of interaction and communication tools, all available within a single user interface.

The VLE comprises two basic functions: (1) interaction between tutors and students, including communication and incidental exchange of information, and (2) content distribution, i.e. online publication, management and retrieval of documents and other information.

Although the VLE could be said to comprise an individual system within the online services of an institution, it should also be considered in the context of wider institutional systems, including:

- *Network accounts*. The VLE is often integrated with student and staff records, allowing for use of an existing network login account to access the VLE.

- *Course records*. The VLE may allow for integration with course records, to provide online courses in parallel with actual taught courses.

- *Institutional portal.* The VLE homepage may also be used as the institutional web portal, providing access to a range of institutional resources, including book-purchasing information, current events or recreational information.

VLEs are also considered in the context of an institutional MLE, or managed learning environment, a term used to describe the entire range of online services provided within an institution, including access to personal data, finance information, credit schemes and library records.

In a recent UCISA report (2003), the role of the VLE is seen in the context of online services within the modern HE institution:

> ... the component(s) within an MLE that provides the 'online' interactions of various kinds, which can take place between learners and tutors ... (p. 8)

Key features

We have already considered early forms of learning technology on the Internet and various approaches to e-learning software, including synchronous tools, such as real-time chat, and asynchronous approaches, such as file exchange.

 We have noted how e-learning systems are typically delivered via the Internet and demonstrate the following key advantages:

- e-learning systems are available online, and may therefore be accessed from any Internet-connected computer;
- e-learning systems allow for interaction and communication between staff and students, typically via the web browser interface;
- e-learning systems may be used to publish and distribute content, including a range of document formats, such as Microsoft Word, Excel and Access, and multimedia formats such as images and audio.

VLEs typically allow for integration with existing user directory systems (such as Microsoft Active Directory), allowing staff and students to log in to the VLE using their normal username and password. Consider this typical model for users on a VLE:

- all users within the institute can log into the VLE using their usual network login (username and password);

- because user accounts are available within the VLE, users can be registered on any number of online courses within the system;

- once a user is registered on an individual site or online course, that user may be allocated the role of either 'staff' (to manage that online course) or 'student' (to view the online course and use interactive features).

Once a user has registered on an online course, there is usually some mechanism or policy to decide the kind of role or status of users within the online course. It is possible within most VLEs to use a range of roles to determine the rights of individual users to view or manage online courses; these roles are defined by varying terminology but are typically similar to the following:

- *Administrator.* The system administrator typically manages the system at the highest level, including actual installation and technical maintenance of server equipment. Administrators manage the appearance and style of the entire VLE and usually liaise with academic staff to organise VLE courses within subject or departmental areas for tutor and student access.

- *Course manager.* This role may be allocated to academic practitioners and academic support staff to develop online courses. This role usually allows the staff member to add or remove documents in an online course and to manage a range of communication tools for interaction with students. The course manager role is usually allocated for individual courses; for example, a tutor's VLE account may have course manager rights for a particular online course, but could have student rights for another course which he or she merely wishes to view.

- *Student.* The student role usually allows for viewing and downloading of course materials, and interaction with other users via communication tools, but not management of the online course. This is the default role that usually applies to any user newly registered on an online course.

- *Other roles.* Sometimes it is possible to allocate other roles within the VLE for particular levels of access, e.g. a 'guest' role may allow access to course documents but not to communication tools.

- *Custom roles.* Some VLEs allow for the creation of custom roles, where levels of access may be specified, e.g. a 'visitor' role, which would allow viewing of specific course areas but prevent access to others.

VLEs often demonstrate a wide range of facilities for interaction and communication, and also allow for sophisticated management of resources within online courses, including search and retrieval tools, cross-linking between VLE content and document editing (e.g. via a word processor) within the VLE itself.

Functions within the VLE may be considered within three key areas:

- *Online course administration.* The organisation of online courses in parallel with actual taught courses and management of user access within online courses.

- *Content management.* The organisation and deployment of online course documents and other information.

- *Communication tools.* This includes collaboration, messaging, file exchange and other forms of interaction between tutors and students.

Online course administration

VLEs typically consist of individual sites corresponding to actual taught courses. Online courses within the VLE may represent an entire programme, such as a Bachelor's degree, a single year within a degree programme or an individual module.

Online courses within the VLE are typically created by administrator staff. Within some VLEs such as Blackboard and WebCT, it is possible to create system areas corresponding to particular departments, providing department-specific access to online courses for staff or student users. It is advisable to customise access to online courses within the VLE to resemble the actual curriculum structure of institutional departments as closely as possible. Consider this hierarchical example for online course organisation:

Departments:

- Art
  - Art and Design BA
  - Art and Design MA
- Humanities
  - English Literature BA
  - History BA
  - Humanities MA

- Science
  - Applied Sciences for Education
  - Science BSc

There are typically two approaches to creating and organising online courses within VLEs, manual and automatic:

- *Manual.* Online courses may be created manually within the VLE by a system administrator, e.g. created incidentally on request from academic staff; additionally, multiple online courses may often be 'bulk' created at the same time. Key information usually required for online course creation includes the course name, course code and optionally a description of course content. Once the online course has been created, tutors or other trained staff may be invited to continue developing the site.

- *Automatic.* Some VLEs provide for integration with existing course records; rather than create online courses on request from tutors, online courses could be created using an automatic process to reflect taught courses by programme, programme-year or individual modules.

Content management

Online courses within the VLE may contain a wide range of document types, typically uploaded or added to the online course by tutors possessing course management rights. Initial development of an online course should involve some liaison and training to ensure the staff member is familiar with the range of VLE tools available to manage online content.

VLEs usually provide a range of document publishing features within online courses, including the following:

- *Basic document upload.* This usually allows for the addition of a wide range of document formats within the online course, including Microsoft Office documents such as Word, Access and Excel. It should be noted by staff that any proprietary document format published online will require the corresponding application to view files; for example, if a student is using the VLE at home and tries to view a Word file, but does not have the Word application installed on their computer, they will be unable to view the file. Luckily, there are free viewers for Microsoft Office and other applications such as 'Adobe Acrobat Reader', which may be downloaded online – see Appendix 1 (Document authoring applications and viewers).

- *Advanced document upload.* Additional options may be available, such as date restrictions to define when documents should be displayed or should stop displaying for user access.

- *Presentation features.* It may be possible to upload documents for sequential viewing in a defined order, providing a learning path when viewing files. Other presentation formats may be uploaded, such as PowerPoint files (for other presentation applications, see Chapter 6).

- *Folders and directories.* In some VLEs such as Blackboard and Learnwise, content may be organised into an hierarchical structure using folders, similar in concept to the Windows Explorer tool. Organisation of content in this way provides effective navigation for retrieving files. Consider this folder structure within an online course:

> Course proforma
> > Module information
> > Learning outcomes
> Staff information
> > Contact details
> Course documents
> > Timetable
> > Session notes
> > Presentations

- *Other options.* A range of other resources may be included in online courses, including JPEG, GIF or BMP image formats, which can display in the web browser, or audio and video files (see Chapter 6). It is also possible to include web addresses (URLs) within the VLE, either within a defined area for web links or alongside other documents.

Increasingly, it is becoming easier to author interactive learning resources for inclusion within the VLE using third-party software; these could comprise a sequential study guide, interactive features or video; later sections of this book will consider the use of alternative third-party tools for authoring learning resources.

Communication tools

VLEs provide a range of communication tools, allowing for interaction between tutors and students. Often, tutors with course manager role may moderate or control the way communication tools are used within a discussion context. Core communication tools within VLEs include the following:

- *Discussion boards.* Discussion boards are also sometimes termed discussion forums or bulletin boards. Discussion boards typically consist of messages and replies to existing messages; for example, a tutor could add a message entitled 'Opinions about lecture 1', and students could then click on that message to view its contents and post a reply message. Initial messages or topics are typically aligned to the extreme left of the display, whilst replies are shown below and indented to the right of initial messages. This method of indenting, or 'threading' messages may be illustrated as follows:

Did you agree with John's views?	Posted by Paul	21/03/03
I agreed with John	Posted by Mike	22/03/03
I disagreed	Posted by Jane	27/03/03
A New Topic!	Posted by Paul	29/03/03
Thank goodness for that!	Posted by Mike	30/03/03

VLE discussion tools are similar to those commonly seen on the Web, but often provide many advanced features, such as message archiving (the ability to hide old messages) or user moderation (to allow a defined student or other user to edit or remove messages). Discussion boards may be used for debate, collaboration or other educational activities, they may also allow for file attachments, e.g. to include Word processed files to elaborate on a short comment.

- *E-mail.* Some VLEs including recent versions of WebCT and FirstClass allow for a fully inclusive e-mail system within the learning environment. The implication here is that staff or student users are able to send and receive e-mails within the VLE interface.

  Alternatively, some VLEs simply allow for registration of an external e-mail address within VLE user record, allowing users to send e-mail within the VLE interface to other VLE users. In this case, recipients must use their normal e-mail software to read the e-mail message.

Students may simply have an option to e-mail tutors from within the VLE interface, or they may be able to create an online address book to contact users. Care should be taken at the administrator level to restrict publication of e-mail addresses where appropriate and to prevent inappropriate use of mass e-mailing (i.e. the ability to e-mail all registered users).

- *File exchange.* Some VLE systems allow for the exchange of files between staff and students. It is often possible to allow students to send files to tutors within a particular online course, or allow collaboration among students to develop a single document. Recent systems, including WebCT, also allow for advanced versioning to provide access to files at various stages of development. Alternative methods of file exchange include use of traditional e-mail attachments and file attachments in discussion board messages.

- *Personal portfolio/homepage.* Some VLEs allow for authoring of a personal homepage or 'portfolio'. In some cases, there may be scope for review by tutors. The portfolio feature may be used to provide a web-based personal development record or curriculum vitae for students. Portfolio components may also be re-used across some VLE systems compliant with Instructional Management System (IMS) standards.

- *File storage.* Some VLE systems provide a personal file repository area, allowing users to save and retrieve files online. This feature was traditionally provided via campus networks, allowing file storage on a personal folder. Unlike a local area network, some VLEs allow for file storage and retrieval operations from any location with Internet access.

- *Chat.* This is the most popular synchronous communication tool among VLEs, allowing for real-time discussions using a simple text interface to exchange messages instantaneously. The main problem with chat is its lack of permanence, but some VLEs such as Blackboard actually provide an archive feature to store the text from a chat session. Chat is of most importance for distance learning or low-contact teaching, where real-time discussions may be held in lieu of traditional class debate. Chat features may also be called 'virtual classroom', and may also provide presentation tools such as a digital whiteboard.

- *Whiteboard.* This tool typically integrates with chat tools and allows for graphical or textual presentations. The Blackboard system's interactive whiteboard is perhaps one of the best examples of this tool, where web pages, PowerPoint slides or VLE content may be displayed in the whiteboard area.

■ *Project collaboration.* Many systems provide project-based features, allowing students to interact using a range of communication tools, such as file-exchange or e-mail. Group features often contain all the main communication features found on the VLE, the main difference being that only group members may access particular group areas.

■ *Assessment tools.* Some VLEs such as Blackboard and WebCT provide an internal assessment feature allowing for the creation of online tests using a range of question types (e.g. multiple answer, fill in the blank, true or false, essay question). Points may usually be allocated for individual questions within the assessment; on completion by individual students, assessment results are automatically recorded and stored in the course management area of the online course. Detailed reporting is also often available, providing general trends or results for individual attempts. Security features such as password protection and time limit could also prevent abuse of assessment features in a controlled environment (e.g. assessments attempted in a timed session on campus). Immediate asssessment feedback or score results may also be available for student viewing.

■ *Survey tools.* These often provide a similar interface and reporting features seen in online assessments, but do not require score allocations.

■ *Other tools.* Online calendars or announcement tools may be available in some VLEs, allowing staff to add events for student notification.

Choosing a VLE

The most important aspect of establishing a VLE is undoubtedly the initial selection process.

A large number of VLEs exist on the market; many possess the full range of features discussed in previous sections, whereas others focus on particular functions. Some VLEs allow for significant integration with other information systems, whereas others either offer minimal integration or require expensive technical consultancy to achieve this.

A wide range of publications and reports have flooded the library and information sectors concerning criteria for the selection of VLEs.

Perhaps the best criteria for VLE selection are reflected in the aims of the host institution, i.e. what are the educational requirements of the organisation? How will the VLE be used?

As an example, consider an HE institute in Wales, where national, regional and internal legislation ensure a responsibility to provide educational resources via the linguistic medium of both Welsh and English.

Undoubtedly, the selection of an institutional VLE in this case will depend on functionality to provide a customisable interface, i.e. the ability for users to select either a Welsh or English 'view' of the system.

In this context, considering the need for flexibility and awareness of organisational demands, it may be worth noting a few common questions for selection of the VLE:

- *What can I afford?* VLE systems, like most software, can be grouped under the general headings of commercial and open source or other not-for-profit agreements. If your institution has insufficient resources to purchase a commercial VLE, there are obvious financial advantages in choosing an open source alternative. Commercial VLEs are often purchased on a renewable yearly licence, almost like 'renting' software, although other factors may be involved such as the number of students within an organisation. Typically, the more students you have the more expensive the licence will be under this arrangement.

- *How long can I afford to spend on system setup?* The deployment of the VLE should be accomplished using standard project management methods. Following installation, a pilot or test period should ensue, followed by a more formal system rollout across the institution. The length of time taken in testing the system and obtaining user feedback will also depend on staff resources, but a substantial period should be allocated for project testing and delivery before launching the VLE as an institutional service.

- *Should we develop our own system?* The costs of developing an in-house VLE depend on internal expertise, particularly in terms of programming skills required to create online applications. It is important to consider that commercial systems such as Blackboard and WebCT have undertaken many years of development and research before reaching their current levels of functionality. Another option when developing an in-house system is to collaborate with partner organisations; this is largely how the Bodington VLE has been implemented recently.

- *What are the benefits of a commercial system?* Commercial systems are usually developed by large software companies, often with substantial expenditure to refine and develop their product via consultation and testing. Commercial VLEs usually come with some technical support, although higher levels of support (e.g. callout support) may require an additional fee. Disadvantages of commercial systems may include lack of scope for customisation (i.e. being 'locked out' of the software development), recurring licence fees and dependence on system vendors over an indefinite time scale. However, commercial VLEs are the most popular approach adopted by HE providers.

- *What are the benefits of a 'free' system?* Open source (i.e. allowing for non-fee-based distribution and modification of software) and other not-for-profit approaches to software distribution present an obvious financial advantage. However, care should be taken to examine legal documentation relating to the software (i.e. are there any usage restrictions?). Additionally, many not-for-profit VLEs provide minimal technical support, and should only be considered in the context of robust system backup and other failure procedures.

- *Which features are the most important?* Core features often cited as the most important aspect of VLEs include the ability for staff to publish documents online easily (including Word, PowerPoint, etc.) and basic communications features such as the ability to e-mail tutors and other users within the interface. This question relates to the kind of online features educational staff are likely to use; part-time or distance learning-based courses may benefit more from real-time communication tools such as chat, whereas courses delivered via conventional class teaching may find document repository and searching tools more useful.

- *Do I need to integrate the VLE with other systems?* Some VLEs allow for integration with existing institutional systems; integration with student records systems may allow for use of the normal network username and passwords to access the VLE. Integration with course records may also allow for dynamic creation of online courses, in parallel with actual taught courses; this could be done at the programme, year or module level. Other possibilities include integration with library management systems, to allow the user to log into the VLE, then view their library record without a second login. Consultation on integration possibilities should occur with VLE vendors at the time of interest, as integration capability is always in flux. Often, integration may require expensive consultancy or systems development, but the results may be worth it.

- *What are the technical staffing requirements?* Staff should be available to install and manage the actual hardware (i.e. server computer running the VLE on the institutional network). Alternatives to in-house technical staff include outsourcing, i.e. obtaining technical support externally, or hosting the VLE with an external organisation.

- *What are the support requirements?* User support is one of the most vital aspects of VLE deployment, including advice and training for academic staff and authoring of support documentation; qualified professional staff should provide these roles. Other staff should be available to provide user support in a front-end capacity, e.g. from an enquiry or library desk.

- Are there any security issues? User logins derived from a standard user directory (such as Microsoft Active Directory) are used to prevent unsolicited access to the system; other management policies can help in delivering a secure system, including configuring the VLE to hide user e-mails and allowing users to display their e-mail address only to known users.

- *What are the long-term risks?* There are a number of risks that should be assessed in choosing a particular VLE, some of which can be investigated by reading reviews and viewing online discussions on VLE issues, such as the Joint Information Systems Committee (JISC) e-mail forums (*http://www.jiscmail.ac.uk*). Care should be taken to research individual systems and assess the difficulties in maintaining a fully operational system without data loss or complications. Another key consideration is long-term support and provider viability; if the VLE company is located abroad, this could cause support problems. Perhaps the biggest financial consideration is the extent to which the institute may become dependent on a licence-based VLE, resulting in an unavoidable regular (and usually incremental) expenditure to retain the system. Loss of a VLE provider may also cause problems for system development and support.

- *What skill levels are required for tutors?* Tutors and other support staff expected to manage online courses will require certain IT skills to operate the VLE. Care should be taken to select a VLE which can be used without in-depth IT expertise. Some staff may already have significant IT skills, and in this case ease of use may be a lesser consideration.

- *What skills levels are required for students?* The VLE should provide an interface which is usable for the majority of students, i.e. requiring minimal training. Students should have basic IT skills prior to using e-learning systems (e.g. web browsers, e-mail). For further training issues, see Chapter 4.

- *How far can the VLE be customised?* The VLE may require customisation to meet requirements within the institution; customisation may include applying the institutional web style, colour or wider customisation, including modification of the VLE front-end to access other web resources.

- *Does the VLE support required language(s)?* In the case of multilingual regions, language customisation may be a critical issue. Some VLEs, such as the Blackboard ML version, allow users to choose the language used for the interface display; most systems allow for customisation of menu items and other navigation text within the VLE display, but this is often insufficient where several languages will be used.

- *How accessible is the VLE?* The VLE should conform to a range of accessibility standards, primarily the WCAG issued by the World Wide Web Consortium. Other industry-standard specifications may be met by the VLE, such as Section 508 of the US Rehabilitation Act (also see Chapter 5).

Some VLEs compared

Although this text does not seek to advocate particular VLE systems or critically evaluate system functionality, it may be worth comparing the main features available in some of the leading VLE systems, including commercial and not-for-profit-based systems. Demonstration accounts and evaluation downloads are often available for the systems discussed; contact details may be obtained by visiting the appropriate website.

Notes

- Most of these VLE vendors provide pre-existing courses or learning resources that may be purchased and uploaded into the respective VLE; many also provide plug-ins, which provide additional system features.

- These web-based systems should typically be viewed using a standard web browser, such as the latest versions of Internet Explorer or Netscape Navigator; a few exceptions do exist, and current recommendations on the best browser to use will be available at the company's web address.

- For interest only, the current uptake of particular VLE systems was recorded by a joint JISC/UCISA survey (2003), with 43.2 per cent of HE institutions using Blackboard, 34.1 per cent using WebCT, 19.3 per cent using FirstClass and 6.8 per cent using Learnwise, with the remainder spread across a range of other systems.

- VLE hardware requirements for hosting on institutional servers are constantly being updated; similarly, pricing and other features are constantly changing. Although the following reviews provide a basic overview of systems, more recent hardware specifications, accessibility support, pricing and other information may be found at respective system URLs or at the Edutools website (*http://www .edutools.com*).

- Current support for Learning Object standards (IMS, SCORM, etc.) may also be found on the CETIS website (*http://www.cetis.ac.uk/ directory/index_html?start=0*).

- Further VLE systems are listed in Appendix 1.

The following criteria have been included in the descriptions:

General

- VLE name
- Company or developer name
- URL (web address)
- Location
- Cost (where available, from the Chest supplier, providing reduced educational licence fees in many cases: *http://www.chest.ac.uk*)
- Brief description.

Content administration

- Content management tools (to organise, search and retrieve documents)
- Assessment tools (interactive 'quiz' tools for student assessment)
- User accounts administration.

Interaction

- Communication tools
- Project/group tools.

Support

- Location of support (is support available locally or abroad only?)
- Support costs (the cost of support in the event of system upgrade etc).

Technical

- Hardware requirements (the latest requirements for running VLEs change regularly, only a rough guide is given here; current detailed requirements should be sought at the vendor's URL at the time of interest)
- Security features (e.g. to restrict access for non-users)
- Integration features (e.g. interoperability with user records or course records)
- Cost of upgrades (are updates included in the normal licence?).

Other features

- Accessibility compliance (for disabled access)
- Multilingual support
- Support for learning object standards (these allow for import and transfer of resources between different VLEs and other e-learning systems; standards include IMS and SCORM)
- Other notes.

The following VLEs are investigated:

1. WebCT
2. Blackboard
3. FirstClass
4. Learnwise
5. Bodington
6. Teknical Virtual Campus

7. Moodle (description contributed by Dan Stowell, University College London).

1. WebCT

General

- *VLE name.* WebCT Campus Edition (version 4.1 at time of review).
- *Company or developer name.* WebCT Inc.
- *URL (web address).* http://www.webct.com.
- *Location of company.* USA.
- *Cost (licence).* £4,500 plus VAT per annum.
- *Brief description.* WebCT provides a web-based learning environment, including calendar features, student homepages, discussion tools, collaboration and document publishing features. WebCT may also be used as a portal, providing access to a range of institutional web resources. An advanced version, WebCT Vista, provides content management features, allowing for file exchange and personal file storage.

Content administration

- *Content management tools.* Allows for document publishing within online courses using customised menus and a hierarchical structure to organise content. Other content management features include student homepages and a group presentation area for collaborative work.
- *Assessment tools.* An interactive assessment feature is available, supporting a range of question formats, with automatic grading; it is also possible to create surveys. The assessment tools include the ability to add equations using the MathML standard.

Interaction

- *Communication tools.* WebCT allows inclusion of discussion forums, 'drop-box' for coursework submission and a complete internal e-mail system. Chat and whiteboard tools are also available for remote communication. The calendar tool allows for announcements, updates on deadlines, online assessments, etc.

- *Project/group tools for students.* WebCT supports a 'note' tool to add memos to individual pages and bookmarks to store shortcuts to resources within the system. A 'My Progress' feature allows students to view how much they have viewed resources (number of discussions posted, pages visited, etc). Group areas are also possible to allow collaborative presentations, file exchange and discussion.

Support

- *Location of support.* USA

- *Support costs.* Basic support is provided within the licence, with additional fees for special support such as installation. '24/7' (i.e. anytime) technical support is provided for an additional fee.

Technical

- *Hardware requirements.* WebCT is available for either a Solaris, Linux or Windows 2000 server – see the URL for the latest detailed server requirements.

- *Security features.* A range of preset system roles are possible. Secure access to WebCT is also possible using Internet protocol (IP) addresses to restrict access to a range of PCs within an organisation. User access may be linked with standard user directory systems (e.g. Active Directory) and authentication systems (see below).

- *Integration features.* Integrates with a range of student record systems and authentication (security) systems such as Kerberos and LDAP (see URL for details).

- *Cost of upgrades.* Included in licence.

Other features

- *Accessibility compliance.* Complies with standard 508 of the US Rehabilitation Act.

- *Multilingual support.* WebCT plug-ins allow for modification of WebCT to support alternative languages.

- *Support for learning object standards.* Supports learning objects developed according to the following standards: IMS Content Packaging 1.1.2, IMS QTI 1.1, IMS Enterprise 1.1 and LRN 2.0.

- *Other notes.* A context-sensitive help tool is provided for most system features.

2. Blackboard

General

- *VLE name.* Blackboard Learning System™ (version 6 at time of review).
- *Company or developer name.* Blackboard Inc.
- *URL (web address).* http://www.blackboard.com.
- *Location of company.* USA.
- *Cost.* depends on student numbers; supply of Blackboard in the UK is under review but may be purchased directly (outside Chest) – see the Blackboard URL for more information.
- *Brief description.* Blackboard provides a web-based learning environment which allows for the creation of online courses using a standard layout, including discussion forums, content publishing, file exchange, assessment and survey tools. The Blackboard collaboration tool provides a combined chat feature with electronic whiteboard, allowing for distance-learning discussions and presentations. An optional addition to Blackboard includes a portal interface that can be customised to provide an institutional web front page with interactive features for departments and integration with other institutional systems. Blackboard is currently the most popular VLE, possibly due to its simple administration interface for tutors and ability to publish a range of content types using a common interface.

Content administration

- *Content management tools.* Blackboard allows for customised online course design, with 'content areas', to publish documents and access communication tools. Folders can be used within content areas to organise documents, similar in concept to Windows Explorer, but represented using appropriate icons for items such as Word documents and web addresses. File storage and exchange are available for students within the groups feature. Although some content management features are present in the standard distribution (e.g. 'course copy' for course site re-use and capability to copy resources across course sites), an optional 'content system' component is available for an additional cost, providing a wide range of content management features and integration with the VLE component.

■ *Assessment tools.* A full assessment and analysis feature is provided within Blackboard, although other third-party assessment tools such as Questionmark may be integrated. Assessments may be managed and stored in a 'pool' area or uploaded to other online courses. The assessment feature is accompanied by a similar survey tool. Results from interactive assessments and surveys are automatically stored in an 'online gradebook' with test results available using various 'views'; survey results are collated on the basis of anonymous entry. The assessment tool also includes a range of security features to ensure tests are undertaken securely. It is also possible to add equations to assessment questions and resource descriptions throughout the system.

Interaction

■ *Communication tools.* E-mail is supported, using either existing e-mail addresses or a complete internal e-mail system. A discussion area is available supporting multiple forums within online courses, and attachments can also be posted to the forums. The chat tool provides two interfaces: a simple 'lightweight chat' and an advanced version with integrated whiteboard for presentations, including the ability to display content within the online course or browse web pages within the whiteboard window. Calendar and announcements tools may also be used to notify students of current events. Announcements may also be posted by administrators at system-wide level.

■ *Project/group tools for students.* Group areas may be defined by tutors, providing a subset of all main communication tools (including chat, file-exchange, discussion board and e-mail). Students may also create homepages. Course-work submission is also possible via a 'digital drop-box'.

Support

■ *Location of support.* UK and European contacts available, but support is mainly US-based.

■ *Support costs.* Some web-based and e-mail support within licence, but additional costs are required for installation and other technical support.

Technical

- *Hardware requirements.* Supports Unix, Linux and Windows NT/2000 servers. See URL for latest hardware recommendations.

- *Security features.* Access to online courses limited by username and password, derived from a standard directory system or using Blackboard's internal database. An 'access code' may be set for individual course sites, allowing self-registration on online courses.

- *Integration features.* Integrates with student record systems such as SITS and authentication systems including LDAP and Kerberos.

- *Cost of upgrades.* Included in licence, but higher levels with increased functionality (e.g. portal, content management system) include an additional cost.

Other features

- *Accessibility compliance.* Blackboard complies with the US section 508 regulations and supports the JAWS text reader for visually impaired users.

- *Multilingual support.* A multilanguage (ML) version of Blackboard is now available, which allows for an alternative language interface. The standard version of Blackboard also allows for textual customisation of buttons and templates.

- *Support for learning object standards.* Blackboard allows for the inclusion of learning objects created according the following standards: SCORM 1.2, IMS Metadata 1.2.1, IMS Content Packaging 1.1.2 and LRN 3.0.

- *Other notes.* Provides scope for 'building blocks', allowing inclusion of Java-based plug-ins for custom features (this requires programming expertise). A wide range of existing 'building block' plug-ins are available, many of which are free of cost from Blackboard.

3. FirstClass

General

- *VLE name.* FirstClass (version 7.1 at time of review).
- *Company or developer name.* Open Text.
- *URL (web address).* http://www.firstclass.com.

- *Location of company.* USA.
- *Cost.* See URL for latest costs.
- *Brief description.* FirstClass has been cited as a VLE because the system provides a broad range of interactive features and communication tools; however, although some scope for document publishing exists, the strength of the system lies in its collaboration and workflow tools; features include a combined e-mail, fax and voicemail system, collaborative online 'conference' areas, shared calendaring, network file storage capacity for students and instant messaging. The FirstClass system is designed to function across many operating systems and platforms, including hand-held PCs (e.g. personal digital assistants). An optional 'enterprise' level also allows for integration with Lotus Notes (content management system) and Microsoft Exchange (e-mail and scheduling system). The FirstClass system includes both a web interface and Windows-based software to access the system remotely; additionally, a telephony system provides telephone access to FirstClass voicemail.

Content administration

- *Content management tools.* The FirstClass system is primarily designed to facilitate communication, but web publishing is also possible via the system homepage and via student homepages.
- *Assessment tools.* None.

Interaction

- *Communication tools.* Provides full e-mail system integrated with fax and voicemail. Also provides discussion forums and real-time instant messaging. Calendar tools allow for collaboration and announcements.
- *Project/group tools for students.* Groups may be defined, allowing for discussion boards, chat and collaboration using an online presentation tool. Students may also create personal homepages.

Support

- *Location of support.* North America and Europe.
- *Support costs.* Maintenance and support can be acquired at the time of purchase and renewed yearly.

Technical

- *Hardware requirements.* See the vendor URL for server platform details.
- *Security features.* Authentication to the FirstClass system may be protected using a username and password. Various permissions may be assigned to users by tutors. FirstClass also provides security for instant messaging, using an encrypted client-server connection to ensure messages are secure.
- *Integration features.* Allows for connection to or migration from the Microsoft Exchange e-mail and calendaring system and Lotus Notes content management system. Also provides an API (application programming interface) for customised authentication integration.
- *Cost of upgrades.* Included as part of the maintenance and support agreement.

Other features

- *Accessibility compliance.* US section 508 compliance.
- *Multilingual support.* English version only.
- *Support for learning object standards.* No formal support, but 'packaged' learning objects could be delivered via message attachments.
- *Other notes.* FirstClass allows for remote access from both the web browser and a Windows application version – although the web version provides increased flexibility, the application version provides more features (e.g. create groups). FirstClass is a widely scaleable platform and able to manage hundreds of thousands of users on a single server (e.g. Open University 250,000 user base). Additionally, FirstClass provides an internal scripting language, allowing for automation of system tasks, such as bulk creation of groups.

4. Learnwise

General

- *VLE name.* Learnwise (version 2 at time of review).
- *Company or developer name.* Granada.
- *URL (web address).* http://www.learnwise.net.
- *Location of company.* UK.

- *Cost.* Licence applies per annum, based on student numbers. Cost is roughly £1k increment per 1,000 users, with a slight reduction for 20,000 users or more, e.g. up to 500 users £2,000, 2,001–3,000 users £6,000.

- *Brief description.* Learnwise is a web-based learning environment with typical communication and discussion tools, based around a student-centred 'personal information manager'. The personal manager interface provides access to online courses, announcements, course progress and student-focused tools, including interactive diary, tasks, file storage area and e-mail.

Content administration

- *Content management tools.* Allows for document publishing within customised online courses. Also provides personal file storage and file exchange.

- *Assessment tools.* Provides assessment tool using a range of question types with results recorded automatically within the system. Questions can include several media types, including video clips and audio.

Interaction

- *Communication tools.* Discussion forums are provided within online courses; a full internal e-mail system or use of external e-mail addresses are supported. Chat and messaging services are also provided.

- *Project/ group tools for students.* Students may author and manage personal homepages. The group feature provides messaging, e-mail and file exchange.

Support

- *Location of support.* UK.

- *Support costs.* Basic support is provided within the licence but additional fees are required for technical call-out.

Technical

- *Hardware requirements.* Windows 2000 or 2003 server. See URL for latest hardware recommendations.

- *Security features.* Usernames and passwords may be defined to provide system access, with capacity for integration with standard student records systems (see below); various roles are also possible to determine levels of access.

- *Integration features.* Supports student records system integration with the Capia, Microcompass and other systems.

- *Cost of upgrades.* Included in licence.

Other features

- *Accessibility compliance.* Complies with World Wide Web Consortium WCAG levels 1 and 2.

- *Multilingual support.* English only.

- *Support for learning object standards.* Supports the following standards: IMS Content Packaging, IMS Metadata, IMS Enterprise, IMS LIP, IMS QTI 1.2, SCORM 1.2 CMI.

5. Bodington

General

- *VLE name.* Bodington.

- *Company or developer name.* University of Leeds.

- *URL (web address).* http://www.bodington.org.

- *Location of company.* University of Leeds, UK.

- *Cost.* Non-commercial.

- *Brief description.* the Bodington system, developed at the University of Leeds, is one of the most popular not-for-profit VLEs used in the UK. The system is web-based and provides a range of features including content publishing, interactive tests, discussion forums and file exchange. Although the system is basically free and currently under development at the University of Leeds, there is very little support available beyond 'bug-requests'. Bodington tends to be used as a basis for developing a VLE using in-house expertise or within large consortiums such as the Yorkshire FE OnLiNM project (Learning in the New Millennium), Oxford University, University of Highlands and Islands, and Manchester University Medical School.

Content administration

- *Content management tools.* Bodington provides the ability to publish and organise content using a 'location'-based menu structure, e.g. Building > Floor > Suite of Rooms > Room. File exchange is also possible between users, including coursework submission via a 'drop-box'.

- *Assessment tools.* Bodington provides support for a number of quiz formats, including multiple-choice and essay questions, with some automatic reporting.

Interaction

- *Communication tools.* Provides discussion forums, an e-mail feature to contact tutors and mailing lists.

- *Project/group tools for students.* Group areas may be created, allowing for discussion forums and coursework submission; permissions may be set to allow students to upload resources within areas, or for students to setup and maintain their own discussion rooms.

Support

- *Location of support.* UK (provided on an 'as is' basis without formal support).

- *Support costs.* Development and maintenance of Bodington requires in-house or other technical support, as Leeds University does not provide comprehensive support beyond 'fixes'.

Technical

- *Hardware requirements.* Linux- or Windows NT-based servers are required. See URL for latest hardware recommendations.

- *Security features.* Allows for a creation of system-based login accounts for system access. Several roles are available to control user access for system features.

- *Integration features.* No formal provision of integration, but system development may be possible. URLs may be added to provide simple integration with other systems (e.g. library management OPAC).

- *Cost of upgrades.* None.

Other features

- *Accessibility compliance.* Complies with World Wide Web Consortium WCAG levels 1 and 2.
- *Multilingual support.* Some menus and system text may be customised; a Spanish version has been translated.
- *Support for learning object standards.* Supports the IMS QTI standard.

6. Teknical Virtual Campus

General

- *VLE name.* Teknical Virtual Campus.
- *Company or developer name.* Teknical (part of Serco Learning).
- *URL (web address).* http://www.teknical.com.
- *Location of company.* UK.
- *Cost.* Variable licence based on student numbers, e.g. £2,900 per annum for up to 1,000 users, £8,000 for up to 5,000 users.
- *Brief description.* The Teknical Virtual Campus provides a web-based learning system which provides student profiles, integrated e-mail and support for web-based conferencing; Teknical also includes an online assessment component, but also allows for integration with the Questionmark online assessment system. A range of third-party resources may be uploaded, including support for resources created using the separately purchased Teknical suite of authoring tools (for learning objects and assessments). Teknical also provides remote hosting as an alternative to local installation, including remote management of hardware, system infrastructure and system backup.

Content administration

- *Content management tools.* Allows for document publishing using customised menu structures; a global content repository is available to re-use and archive resources; it also includes a content development tool (internal word processor) to author documents within the system. An optional editing tool is also available (for separate purchase) for the creation of learning objects (IMS/SCORM compliant content).

- *Assessment tools.* The question design wizard allows for creation of interactive tests, with automated scoring and results recording.

Interaction

- *Communication tools.* Includes a calendar tool, chat feature, discussion forums and private messaging for users.
- *Project/group tools for students.* Group areas may be defined with file exchange, chat, calendar tool and collaborative document authoring.

Support

- *Location of support.* UK.
- *Support costs.* Approximately £350 per day of support.

Technical

- *Hardware requirements.* Teknical requires the Windows operating system with Internet Explorer 6 for clients (end-users); server requirements include Windows 2000 or 2003 server. See URL for latest hardware recommendations.
- *Security features.* Allows for user login using integration with a range of standard student records systems.
- *Integration features.* Allows for integration with several standard student records systems including Capia, SITS and Fretwell Downing.
- *Cost of upgrades.* Included with licence.

Other features

- *Accessibility compliance.* None stated.
- *Multilingual support.* None stated.
- *Support for learning object standards.* Supports IMS Metadata 1.2.1, IMS Content Packaging 1.1.2, IMS QTI 1.1 and SCORM. Teknical also provides all the National Learning Network (NLN) learning objects (*http://www.nln.ac.uk*) via central servers so that all hosted clients (using the hosting option) have access to the NLN repository.

7. Moodle

General

- *VLE name.* Moodle (version 1.2.1 at time of writing).
- *Company or developer name.* Open source; prime developer is Martin Dougiamas.
- *URL (web address).* http://www.moodle.org.
- *Location.* Prime developer's location is Perth, Australia.
- *Cost.* Free (it is open source; consultancy, installation and development work can be bought in from providers such as *http://www .moodle.com*).
- *Brief description.* Moodle is a free, open-source VLE that provides many of the features of WebCT (part of the motivation for its creation was dissatisfaction with WebCT). It offers many 'modules' including quiz, survey, discussion, assignments, chat, journal, workshop, as well as 'filters' which automatically convert (for example) offensive language into **** or MP3 web addresses into streaming media players. A Moodle 'course' can be focused on topics, or around a discussion area (Moodle claims a 'strong grounding in social constructionist pedagogy'). Moodle is surprisingly easy to install because it runs on an 'ordinary' PHP/MySQL-enabled server, and configures itself largely automatically.

Content administration

- *Content management tools:*
  - Online file management interface for uploading/managing files for a course.
  - Most text entry areas (resources, forum postings, journal entries, etc.) can be edited using an embedded WYSIWYG HTML editor (internal word processor).
  - 'Search' box allows a user to search a course's discussion forums.
  - 'Glossary' tool.
- Assessment tools:
  - 'Quiz' module provides facility for creating and administering online tests using a variety of question formats (MCQ, short-answer, numerical, etc.).

- 'Assignment' module allows the teacher to request that each student submits a file (e.g. a word-processed document or a spreadsheet) for grading.

■ *User accounts administration.* Moodle supports a range of authentication mechanisms (e.g. LDAP, POP3, NNTP, external database, verify-by-e-mail). Each course can optionally be given an 'enrolment key' to restrict access.

Interaction

■ *Communication tools.* Discussions are integral to Moodle, and can be specified as the main focus for a given course (i.e. the course 'homepage') if desired. A 'Chat' module is also available. No 'e-mail' feature is provided – Moodle tends to assume that users already have e-mail accounts. Students are encouraged to build an online profile including photos and descriptions.

■ *Project/ group tools.* 'Workshop' module, 'Journal' module.

Support

■ *Location of support.* Support is mainly through the community discussion at moodle.org. The creator of Moodle (and thus, the physical location of moodle.org) is from Australia. Very little third-party support is available at present.

■ *Support costs.* Free via community discussion at moodle.org, although of course this comes with no guarantees of support. Support/consultancy may be purchased from moodle.com.

Technical

■ *Hardware requirements.* Moodle can be installed on almost any platform that supports PHP (e.g. Unix, Linux, Windows). Requires one database (which can be shared with other network systems).

■ *Security features.* A user must be logged in, in order to use a course, and user authentication can come from one of a variety of sources, as specified by the administrator (see below). Moodle allows 'guest' login, and each course can choose to allow or disallow guest access. Each course can also have an 'enrolment key' specified.

■ *Integration features.* For user authentication, it will integrate with LDAP, NNTP, POP3 or a specified external database.

■ *Cost of upgrades.* Nil.

Other features

- *Accessibility compliance.* Uses a simple 'low-tech' browser interface (it does not seem to use any JavaScript or 'dynamic HTML', and makes very little use of frames).

- *Multilingual support.* Moodle comes with more than 34 languages built in – the user can choose which language the interface uses.

- *Support for learning object standards.* Standards-based import and export (SCORM for courses, QTI for quizzes) are being developed, but are not present in the current 'production' version.

- *Other notes*: There is an online help tool for most system features. Extra modules are available for free download at *http://moodle .org/download/modules* (e.g. 'Wiki' module, 'HotPot' module for integrating quizzes created by Hot Potatoes software)

VLE examples

During winter 2003/2004, the author distributed an informal question-naire examining VLE use across UK HE institutions; the results provide several brief but interesting case studies. See Appendix 2 for the original questionnaire.

The respondents included:

- University of the West of England, Bristol
- University of Durham
- University of Brighton
- City University (London)
- University of Surrey
- Lancaster University
- University of Bradford.

University of the West of England, Bristol (~25,000 students)

The Blackboard system was purchased at this institution in 2002, following initial experiments developing in-house VLEs. Blackboard was selected based on criteria for ease of use and compatibility with the institute's student records system. The VLE was installed internally, using institute expertise.

The institutional Learning and Teaching Strategy drives VLE development; core systems management is provided by a team of six individuals, with two academic staff providing pedagogical design and advocacy. Representatives from each academic faculty also provide e-learning coordination, liaising with the VLE team.

At present, the VLE is primarily used for online publishing, with growing use for communications features. Approximately one-third of institutional modules have a presence on the VLE.

Shortage of time was cited as the main challenge for academic practitioners to grasp the new technology, although the deployment of Blackboard was considered an important step to facilitating flexible models for teaching within the institution.

University of Durham (~10,000 students)

The University of Durham began using the Blackboard online learning system (version 5) in 2000, adding the advanced Community Portal system in 2003 and more recently moving to version 6. Previously, departments within the institute had used basic web page authoring tools, with development expertise drawn from staff across the institute.

Blackboard had been selected as it was considered a flexible system that would allow a range of educational uses, and for interface customisation to suit the institute style.

Durham had been involved in a collaborative e-learning project before purchasing Blackboard, using a bespoke VLE developed by the University of Newcastle. This provided valuable experience both when first evaluating competing products and later during the deployment of Blackboard. Although consultancy for installing Blackboard was considered, the Learning Technologies Team supported by staff from the Systems Group were able to establish the system internally.

Uptake on the VLE has been substantial, with each department achieving some e-learning activity. The system has been expanded using Java building blocks, including custom-built news feeds, evaluation tools, content types and portal modules.

The VLE is integrated with the student records system (SCT Banner) and users authenticate using a Lightweight Directory Authentification Protocol (LDAP) against Active Directory.

Further integration has been achieved by linking to parts of the library OPAC and search tools on existing university intranet pages. Gradually these links are being replaced with fully integrated solutions written in Java.

The deployment of the VLE is driven by the institutional learning and teaching strategy, with consultation from individual departments. Although the majority of system management and user training is undertaken by the Learning Technologies Team, unofficial 'champions' also exist within academic departments to coordinate e-learning activities.

University of Brighton (~17,000 students)

This institution installed Blackboard in 2002. Previously, web authoring and an intranet had been used to deliver web content. The installation of Blackboard was achieved internally without Blackboard consultancy. Criteria for the selection of the VLE included ease of use and scope for communication tools, including e-mail, integrated online assessment and group features.

Since deployment, Blackboard has been configured to provide integration with student records and provides links to the library management system.

The institutional learning and teaching strategy includes support for e-learning and learning technologies. Within the Learning Technologies group, three staff provide core system management and development, with pedagogical support from five academic staff and liaison from e-learning champions across the institute.

Uptake of Blackboard has been achieved across over 50 per cent of institute modules; the VLE has also provided important support for part-time study through communications and content publishing features.

City University (London) (~12,000 students)

This institution purchased the WebCT system in 2002 in the enhanced Vista version, and implementation was achieved by September 2003.

Previous VLE experiments included basic web authoring within academic departments. The criteria for selection of WebCT was cited as pedagogical functionality, ease of use and reputation. The WebCT company was involved in installing the system with some in-house technical support. Integration has also been achieved with the Strategic

Information Technology Services (SITS) student record system and a single sign-on, allowing for access to WebCT and other intuitional systems following a single user login.

E-learning is supported within the Learning and Teaching strategy, with over 140 modules present on the system. The e-learning team (five staff) provide a range of pedagogical, technical and user support for academic staff.

Issues in delivering the VLE included resource problems and concern over the growing reliance on technology by academic departments; however, the system was considered an important tool in providing flexible models of teaching, innovation and efficiency.

University of Surrey (~12,000 students)

This institution purchased the WebCT Vista system in 2003, in partner ship with its sister institution at Roehampton. Installation of the VLE was achieved in-house by IT services with some consultancy from WebCT.

Key criteria for selection of the VLE were the provision of good support for group-based learning activities, compatibility with existing management information systems to allow the creation of an MLE and the ability to support multiple institutions (e.g. partner colleges) from a single installation. The system was tested for accessibility compliance.

Pedagogical support and staff development relating to teaching developments within the VLE are provided by the central, five-strong 'E-learning Team', who work collaboratively with academic staff. The benefits of discussion and other communication tools are considered vital in the support of collaborative student learning both on blended and on distant-learning courses.

The university is also encouraging all schools to develop their individual e-learning strategy that links to their overall learning and teaching strategy and priorities, with internal funding made available to support this approach; this is already proving beneficial in coordinating activity and resources within schools.

Lancaster University (~10,000 students)

Lancaster had purchased the Lotus Notes system in 1993, now IBM's Lotus Domino. This system provides a range of content management, document publishing and communications tools, which have been integrated to form the web-based Lancaster University Virtual Learning Environment (LUVLE).

The system was installed and developed in-house, with several research projects providing impetus for development. More recently, integration has been undertaken with a range of other systems, including the library management system, student information system and user login integration using Microsoft's Active Directory.

Several full- and part-time staff provide core system and e-learning support for academic staff; a key support role for students is played by departmental administrators, who assume some system administration functions. The Domino system is also linked to the (developing) institutional e-learning strategy.

Use of the Domino system within academic departments stands at around 50–60 per cent of modules, with ease of use cited as the main reason for the success of this system.

University of Bradford (~10,000 students)

The University of Bradford IT team installed the Blackboard system during 2001. Integration is also about to be achieved with the SITS student records system for user logins.

With a large part-time student population (2,319), the importance of communication and other distant-learning features were cited as important aspects of the VLE, where placement support for vocational learners is essential. Although the VLE is currently well utilised by two academic schools (Health Studies and Management), learning technology support for e-learning activities is also available across the institute. Concerns regarding system reliability have been raised in the past, but system uptake has increased and an e-learning strategy is in development.

Further issues in deploying and managing the VLEs are discussed in the next chapter.

3

Managing the virtual learning environment

Deployment

This chapter discusses general practical issues surrounding the initial deployment, service delivery and management of the VLE.

Initial installation of the VLE will depend largely on qualified technical personnel within the institute; this expertise may be present within the Information Services area or another IT department. VLE installation may also require external consultancy, particularly if internal expertise is unavailable for particular platforms or systems; most VLE companies provide consultancy, although this usually incurs an additional fee to the actual system purchase.

Following installation and technical setup, the administration and service delivery of the VLE is usually the remit of an information services style department, or may be managed by several closely related teams.

There are usually three important areas of expertise required for VLE deployment:

- *Technical skills.* Including the ability to install, configure and maintain the VLE software and server hardware. This role also includes integration with other institute systems, including course and user records. This technical activity is sometimes the responsibility of a separate IT team.

- *User and course records management.* This includes regular creation and maintenance of user records, creation of online courses and organisation of courses for user access. This role is typically undertaken by Information Services personnel, and usually involves liaison with both academic staff (for course issues) and technical staff (for system integration issues.)

- *Training and user support.* This role includes all user support functions, and may be spread across a range of professional and support staff; activities include advocacy and user-awareness of the VLE, staff and student training, and incidental user support. Authoring of brochures, manuals and online support materials is also an important support activity.

The process of VLE purchase and deployment should be undertaken as a managed project, with contingency plans to meet changing circumstances. The VLE should be provided initially on a pilot or test basis prior to formal service delivery. An example of a managed VLE project could comprise the following stages:

1. VLE procurement discussed at institutional level, possibly forming part of strategic objectives or planning.
2. Internal resources for VLE deployment defined, including financial and existing personnel capacity, with consideration for additional staff appointments.
3. Process started to define and formalise the team for core deployment and support of the VLE.
4. VLE procurement group assembled to facilitate initial VLE selection (comprising core VLE deployment team, potential stakeholders from Information Services, academic departments and other senior institutional staff).
5. VLE procurement group investigate products available, including costs, current e-learning research and other issues for e-learning in the HE sector.
6. Consultation with key stakeholders, e.g. academic department heads, to establish criteria for procurement.
7. VLE products evaluated using selection criteria.
8. VLE procurement group present suitable systems for consideration, followed by demonstrations from vendors.
9. Decision taken for VLE purchase.
10. Negotiation with VLE company or supplier to set exact costs, support provision and resolve technical issues for installation and integration (defined using an 'invitation-to-tender' style document).

11. VLE server hardware and software obtained according to vendor recommendations (unless service will be hosted on an external organisation's server).

12. VLE server computer and software installed on institute network by core VLE team, possibly with call-out support of vendor or other internal IT expertise. Other systems integration may occur at this point (e.g. student records system).

13. VLE strategy group established to coordinate VLE deployment, including core VLE team members and other stakeholders across institution.

14. Strategy for deployment of the VLE defined, including definitions for the role of core VLE team staff, other internal staff (e.g. academic roles) and initial user awareness and induction.

15. Initial pilot of VLE system provides training and access to VLE for restricted academic practitioners and students.

16. Pilot feedback used to enhance or develop VLE.

17. General notification of VLE availability to academic staff across institution, including details to obtain training for staff and students.

E-learning strategy

The provision of the VLE should be driven by appropriate strategy and planning.

Strategic issues in deploying the VLE should complement the institutional 'learning and teaching strategy', which may have an e-learning component.

It is possible that the impetus to obtain a VLE may arise from existing strategic planning; however, it is important that an appropriate VLE procurement group is defined to ensure relevant stakeholders have a voice in the initial selection of the VLE.

Initially, a VLE procurement group should be established to consider VLE products available, define costs, examine resource requirements and discover the experience of other institutions in delivering the VLE. Consultation may also occur within the institute via questionnaires or workshops to discover the needs of academic practitioners.

Following selection of the system by the procurement group, a VLE strategy group should be established to develop the long-term strategic agenda of VLE delivery.

A VLE strategy document should also be compiled, to define the status and aims of the VLE system within the institute and demonstrate how VLE strategy corresponds to wider strategies, such as learning and teaching strategy or information services strategy. The VLE strategy could also define stakeholders for VLE activity, including the VLE deployment team and other staff, such as pedagogical expertise.

A related, but separate, policy and procedure document, probably defined by VLE deployment staff may also be useful in early stages of VLE delivery, defining methods for online course management, the operational role of staff and procedures for training and user support. Both the VLE strategy document and policy document will provide a useful reference for discussion and advocacy for the VLE system across the institute.

System integration

Many VLE systems allow for integration with other core institutional systems. Although integration is a technical subject and largely beyond the remit of this text, it may be useful to discuss some of the common approaches and terms used in integration.

The most common aims of integration are as follows:

- *User login.* Many VLEs allow for integration with existing user databases, allowing users to log into the VLE using their normal institute username and password; this login method is often very secure, because logins are unique per user; additionally, only one network login must be remembered to access the VLE and other network systems.

- *Online courses.* Course records may be integrated with the VLE automatically to provide online courses in parallel with actual courses, at the programme, year or module level. Manual creation of individual courses is the most common alternative to integration, but this can be time consuming and prone to inaccuracy.

- *Other systems.* In some cases, VLEs allow for integration with library management systems or other web-based communication systems, such as Microsoft Exchange or Lotus Domino. Simple hyperlinks may also provide access to any local or external web-based resource within the VLE interface.

A range of current technical standards and systems exist that allow for integration; it is useful to have a basic awareness of these standards to evaluate potential for systems integration:

- *Directory services.* These are database systems, which allow user accounts to be shared with other networked systems. Directory services may contain user records, including name, e-mail and department. Directory services may be considered as a networked database, which may allow for administration by support staff via an interface or a linked system. Common directories include Active Directory (a Microsoft server component) and Novell Directory Services or NDS (on the Novell Netware server). VLE vendors typically indicate which directory standards are required to integrate with user records.

- *Authentication services.* These are security systems that act as a kind of gatekeeper to networked resources, querying a user password or username with the appropriate record on a directory service. Common authentication services include Kerberos and LDAP. VLE companies usually indicate which authentication standards are supported for integration with user logins. Authentication may also be set to allow single sign-on, i.e. to allow a user to access multiple distinct online resources following only a single login. If integration is present within a user directory, but not an authentication system, then users may log in using their normal network username but not their normal password; in this case, a password must be set for users within the VLE system. However, where user authentication integration is present, the user may log in using the normal password, because the authentication system has allowed the VLE to query the remote system for the password.

- *Library management systems.* Some VLEs allow for integration with library system records, enabling users to query or update records from within the VLE interface, or to create reading lists based on library system searches. This integration is often possible using basic hyperlinks to the appropriate library catalogue (OPAC).

- *Student records systems (SRSs).* These are used to organise and supply core user information, including personal details, finance, course information and course results. Some VLEs may integrate with an SRS system to provide a personalised interface for users or display actual course grades. Examples of SRSs include SITS and SCT Banner.

Configuring the VLE

Many aspects of the VLE may typically be customised or configured without significant technical expertise.

The appearance of the VLE interface may often be modified to reflect the style of existing institutional systems; access to online courses may also be organised according to institute schools, departments and subjects.

Configuration possibilities may include the following:

- *Interface style.* Including institutional logo, colours or typeface.

- *Portal.* Customisation of the VLE interface as a portal to access other institutional web resources.

- *Organisation of online courses.* Arranging access to online courses by school or subject to reflect academic structures.

- *Course template.* A template may be created for the creation of all online courses using a standard layout, including font colour, style and navigation menu to access course materials. The template could include pre-defined content for inclusion in every online course, including links to the library catalogue, online databases or electronic journals. Templates may also be used to control the names of menu items for course content, or remove links to unused features.

- *Customisation of features and tools.* The appearance and behaviour of system features may often be modified, e.g. determining the ability of students to create home pages or personal profiles, or the ability of staff to create incidental student accounts.

- *Customisation of roles.* System roles may often be modified to allow or restrict access to features, e.g. modification of the 'course manager' role to disallow viewing of student details, or modification of the 'student' role to prevent modification of user information on the system.

- *Customisation of language.* Some VLEs, such as Blackboard ML (special multi-language version), allow for the selection of language within the VLE interface and features. Other systems may allow for renaming of navigation features and buttons using a desired language; modification of this latter kind does not usually allow for modification of some pop-up messages, help files and other occurrences of the original system language.

Managing users and courses

Most VLEs provide tools to manage user accounts at a range of levels. Assuming integration is present with user records, very little manual accounts administration may be required; however, management of user access to individual online courses may require additional administration.

User management for system administrators

The advantage of integration with an existing user database (for students and staff) means that the entire body of users may access the VLE using their existing username; with authentication integration, users may also use their usual network password. This means that most user accounts need not be created on the VLE by hand and users may simply log into the VLE to access the main interface for online courses. Even when user directory integration is present, the VLE will usually store internal accounts for all users, simply querying the common network password on the user directory system.

Accounts may also be created on an incidental basis for external or other special users; incidental accounts are usually stored on the VLE database itself and require a username and password set by the VLE administrator (not derived from integrated user records). The ability to create incidental accounts in this way is useful to provide access for external or other users lacking an internal network account.

Manual creation and removal of user accounts on the VLE may be necessary for systems without integration, where all users will require a manually created account; a batch tool is sometimes available to create users in bulk, using a simple text file listing user details in an appropriate format.

Removal of user accounts is usually possible via an automatic or manual method; this feature is vital to remove users who have completed courses or have otherwise left the institute.

Most of these user account operations should be performed by a VLE system administrator only, because the creation and removal of user accounts is a global issue, i.e. a user may possess an account to log into the VLE, and may require access to a number of distinct online courses representing different modules. Where the student completes one module but continues another, the user should be removed from the relevant online course; however the entire user account itself should not be removed, as this would terminate access to the entire system. This 'high'-level user management should be restricted to VLE staff or others working in a defined administrator capacity.

Another feature of this level of account management is the definition of system roles. It is often possible to define users using roles similar to the following:

- *System administrator.* Responsible for technical and high-level system administration.

- *Accounts administrator.* Allows access to user accounts features, but not other administrator features.

- *User (or non-administrator).* This role will provide ordinary access to the system as a user, without any system management access. Students and tutors will typically have this role. However, a tutor with this system role may be given a 'course manager' role specific to an individual online course.

User management for tutors

Assuming all institute users may log into the VLE using existing login information, we then have the problem of providing access to individual online courses.

The management of online courses may be undertaken by core VLE staff, but could also be undertaken by academic practitioners or other academic support staff who have undertaken appropriate VLE training.

Academic staff managing online courses should be registered on the appropriate online course; they may be allocated a 'course manager' or similar role to manage content and supervise student access within individual online courses.

Typically, tutors may add or remove students using course management tools. It should be noted that when a student has been removed from an online course, this does not necessarily mean their VLE account has been deleted, and the user may continue to log in and access other online courses.

Some systems also allow for self-registration by students to access online courses. The Blackboard VLE allows for an 'access code', which may be distributed to VLE users to allow registration on individual online courses; in the Blackboard VLE the user enters a 'course catalogue' and selects the desired course name (within an appropriate department area). After clicking on an 'enrol' button, the student is asked for the 'access code', and the student may then access the required course site from a 'my courses' area.

Importantly, students who have completed courses should be removed from the relevant online course.

Methods for the creation and removal of user accounts by administrators and user management by tutors or other support staff should ideally be documented in a VLE 'policy and procedures' document.

Online course management

The organisation and management of online courses has already been discussed earlier, but it is worth considering the importance of liaison between VLE staff and academic practitioners in this area.

Online courses are typically created from a standard template, but customisation of new courses is usually necessary. When planning a new online course with tutors, care should be taken to consider the aims or emphases of the academic practitioner and their teaching requirements. Part-time or distance-learning-based courses may require better coverage for communication tools, with obvious shortcuts provided within menu navigation for otherwise hidden features.

The online course navigation menu may require customisation to suit the structure of the course or module, with appropriate terms defined for menu items to access particular content areas, such as 'module proforma' or 'reading list'.

General organisation of online courses within the system is also a significant issue; care should be taken to arrange links to online courses to reflect the actual academic structure of the institute, using actual department names and, where possible, using appropriate institutional terms, such as 'school', 'programme' or 'module'.

Some US-derived systems may use terminology peculiar to the US education system, but it is possible in most systems to change this where required to suit local terms, e.g. 'faculty' becomes 'school'.

Academic practitioners will have the option to perform a wide range of course management functions, typically including the following:

- add/remove users (within individual online courses only);
- send e-mail to students;
- create groups for project-based activity;

- post announcements, deadlines and other current events;
- use coursework submission tools to receive student files (usually called a 'drop-box');
- add a range of content types, including Microsoft Office files (e.g. Word, Excel), Adobe Acrobat (PDF) documents, images, URLs (web links) or any other file type;
- create interactive tests for student completion and view assessment grades;
- deliver interactive sessions using chat or whiteboard tools for distance learning.

Publishing on the VLE

Although it is possible to upload a range of file types to the VLE, including Microsoft Office and other document formats, care should be taken to consider a number of issues.

File size

If the document you have uploaded is larger than 2 megabytes (2,048 kilobytes) and the student is using a modem Internet connection (with a maximum bandwidth of 56 kilobits per second), it is likely the download may take quite a long time. Few home users have the faster but more expensive broadband Internet access, so care should be taken to reduce file size as much as possible.

To discover the size of your file, open Windows Explorer. Go to the Start button > Run > Type 'explorer' > click OK, browse to your file, which will probably be on your hard drive (C:), the floppy drive (A:) or another drive letter.

You will see the file listed in the right-hand window, and the 'size' is indicated in KB (kilobytes), with 1024 KB equal to 1 MB (megabyte). Note: if the file size is not listed, try clicking on the file with the right mouse button, and then select 'Properties'.

If the file is over 2 MB, you should try to reduce the file size to ensure faster downloading; the ideal file size is equal to or below 500 KB.

Steps to reduce file size include:

- Remove unnecessary images.

- Resample images in a graphics program such as Paint Shop Pro, by reducing the level of resolution (PPI, pixels per inch), reducing colours used or reducing the actual image dimensions (canvas size).

- Make sure 'fast save' is disabled in Microsoft Office applications, such as Word or PowerPoint, as this simply adds extra unnecessary file information every time you 'save'. In your Microsoft Office application, go to: Tools > Options > Save > untick Allow fast saves.

- Remove other supporting files, such as clipart.

- Split larger documents up into smaller ones, e.g. Chapter 1.doc, Chapter 2.doc, allowing users to choose required files for download.

- Try not to use the BMP (bitmap) image format, as this takes up considerable file space. If you are using a digital camera or scanner, try selecting GIF (graphical interchange format) or JPEG (joint photographic experts group) formats, or convert your files to one of these standards using a graphics program such as Paint Shop Pro.

- Remove background images, themes or special features, such as PowerPoint transitions between slides, as these all take up extra file space.

File formats

Care should also be taken to ensure students may easily access document formats used on the VLE. Although it is possible to upload any kind of file on the VLE, it is usually necessary for users to open uploaded files using an appropriate application.

Web browsers, such as Internet Explorer and Netscape Navigator, allow for viewing document formats such as Word and Acrobat within the actual web browser window, but the respective applications (e.g. Microsoft Word, Adobe Acrobat Reader) are still required on the user's computer to view these files.

Within the institutional library or IT lab, common applications will already be installed on computers, so that viewing a range of file formats is possible. However, students at home may not have the relatively expensive Microsoft Office suite or other applications required to view these files (students should obtain the free Microsoft Word or PowerPoint viewers available – see Appendix 1, document applications and viewers).

It may be useful to provide access to URLs in help documents for free file viewers such as Adobe Acrobat Reader and the Microsoft Office Suite.

Online course structure

When publishing documents online, academic staff should be aware of tools within the VLE for organising or structuring their material. Some systems, such as WebCT and Blackboard, provide the ability to separate documents using 'folders' (and subfolders) with defined labels or names. Consider this example:

'Course Notes' (area within navigation menu in online course):

- Lectures
  - Presentations
    - PowerPoint presentation 1.ppt
    - PowerPoint presentation 2.ppt
  - Handouts
    - Handout 1.doc
    - Handout 2.doc
- Study notes
  - Coursework
    - Coursework 1.doc
    - Coursework 2.doc
  - Reading list
    - Bibliography.doc

Document searching and metadata

Some VLEs allow for advanced content searching and retrieval, including tools to search within either the current online course or a range of courses. Searching may be assisted by document categories or descriptions added during document upload; for example, the Blackboard system allows for metadata, i.e. descriptive statements including name of author, document title or description. Inclusion of accurate metadata, possibly using an authority file of formal terms, such as module names or subjects may enhance document searching within the VLE.

Templates and generic content

Templates

It may be possible to add a range of generic materials within the VLE, using a predefined template or several templates for custom purposes, e.g. an art school template, a science template.

The template may be populated with a range of content, including basic help on using the VLE or links to educational resources, such as reading lists, electronic journals, study information or direct links to the library catalogue.

Department-specific templates could also include subject-based resources, such as links to relevant academic websites, or online catalogue searches to display catalogue entries for particular keywords (e.g. a search for 'history' within a web-based library catalogue would display a range of results, and the URL of this results page could be copied directly from the address bar of the web browser and added as a direct hyperlink within an online course).

Repositories

A range of methods may be used to maintain a repository or store of generic resources, which may be reused throughout the VLE across all online courses.

Although online courses must typically be maintained individually, some systems allow for a common resource area, which can be accessed from other online courses.

Repositories may also be structured or organised using folders, providing a hierarchical model to classify or categorise items.

The following resources could be used in a repository area:

- former essay papers, arranged by subject or year;

- URLs to generic study guides, arranged by competence or skill;

- URLs for subject-based websites, arranged by discipline or subject;

- an image collection, arranged by topic or theme.

It may also be possible to provide a repository of interactive assessments or individual assessment questions, which may be accessed and uploaded into any online course.

The advantages of re-using and maintaining resources within a common area means that a range of online sites may access resources without maintaining them individually; for example, rather than re-uploading the same file to 30 online courses, this file could be added to the common repository area or site, and individual courses could then access the new file, using a hyperlink to the repository.

VLEs and the electronic library

We have already discussed how integration is possible across a range of institutional systems within the VLE; however, it is perhaps useful to consider wider possibilities for the VLE as an interface for library and information services.

Traditional library services are increasingly provided in an electronic and online context. Early efforts to deliver printed databases and indexes via the Internet (e.g. BUBL – see below) provided the impetus for the later explosion in online information resources available via the World Wide Web.

Information sources available on a local area network or via the World Wide Web may be accessed from within the VLE interface using a basic hyperlink (web address). A few possibilities for links of this kind could include:

- *Library OPAC.* The library management interface is increasingly web-based, providing for almost seamless integration with the VLE. Traditional text-based OPACs, based on telnet, may also be accessed from the VLE via a hyperlink, but the format for a telnet URL will be slightly different (e.g. *telnet://myopac.someplace.ac.uk*).

- *Internal intranet.* Students or staff may access a password-protected user-only intranet containing institutional, personal or course-based information, possibly based on a student records system such as SITS.

- *Web directories.* Information service staff or academic practitioners may create lists or directories of links to useful web resources, including academic based web pages, study guides or links to locally developed web resources. Web directories may be easily created within online courses, often allowing for hierarchical categorisation of links using folders. Web directories could also be created outside the VLE using web authoring software and hosted on a separate server, with access provided from the VLE using a simple hyperlink to the index page.

- *PC and IT equipment booking.* It may be possible to link to an internal web-based booking system to use IT facilities such as scanners or computers. Systems of this kind are usually developed using internal expertise. A similar system may allow for room booking for academic staff.

- *Academic web pages.* Access may be provided within the VLE to traditional websites, possibly developed within academic departments using web editing software such as FrontPage.

- *Other communication systems.* Links could be added to other communications systems within the institute, such as Microsoft Exchange or Lotus Domino, providing shared calendars, e-mail and other collaboration tools.

- *Content management systems.* Although the VLE typically provides focus for educational activity, other content management systems may allow staff easily to publish documents online for institutional purposes (such as personnel information, health and safety or other institutional policies).

- *Internet portals.* These include categorised indexes of links on the World Wide Web; portals or 'gateways' often provide a hierarchal or category-based interface to access resources, including academic subjects or disciplines. Well-known portals include RDN (the Resource Discovery Network: *http://www.rdn.ac.uk*), BUBL (The Bulletin Board for Libraries: *http://www.bubl.ac.uk*) and HERO (Higher Education and Research Opportunities: *http://www.hero.ac.uk*).

- *Subject-specific portals.* These provide access to subject-based resources on the World Wide Web; popular subject portals include ADAM (The Art, Design, Architecture & Media Information Gateway: *http://www.adam.ac.uk*), BizEd (Business Resources: *http://www.bized.ac.uk*) and ELDIS (natural and built environment information sources: *http://nt1.ids.ac.uk/eldis*). Also see a gateway to e-learning information maintained by the author (E-learning Information Portal: *http://elearning.draigweb.co.uk*).

- *Government information sources.* Many government websites provide statistical information, legislative documents and other resources, e.g. the ONS (Office of National Statistics: *http://www.ons.gov.uk*).

- *Online abstract and full-text databases.* Some full-text databases provide not-for-profit access to citation information or actual full-text articles, whereas others require a subscription fee to access resources, e.g. MEDLINE (Health abstracts), OCLC ArticleFirst (general resources accessed by subject: *http://www.oclc.org*) and ISI Web of Knowledge (*http://wok.mimas.ac.uk*).

- *RSS news* (Rich Site Summary or Really Simple Syndication). RSS news feeds are documents written in XML, a web mark-up standard containing classes of information, e.g. title, item, date, description and summary. RSS news documents are widely available on the Internet dealing with a diverse range of cultural and academic topics. Access to RSS documents is possible using an RSS reader (or aggregator), either in the form of a Windows application (such as the 'RSS Reader': *http://www.rssreader.com*) or use of a web-based application for integration with existing web resources (e.g. using Javascript or ASP). Selected RSS news addresses for use within RSS applications are listed on Yahoo, and may also be accessed directly (*http://news.yahoo.com/rss*).

Security and abuse

Although it is beyond the remit of this text to explore detailed technical issues in VLE systems, it may be useful to discuss some of the more practical methods for delivering a secure service when deploying the VLE.

Internet security prevents access to networked resources by unauthorised users, and is a vital component of the VLE. Typical methods for ensuring VLE security include:

- *User accounts/authentication.* Integration with a user records database (such as Active Directory) and an authentication system (such as LDAP) should allow for use of the normal network username and password to access the VLE, restricting access to individuals without an institutional network account.

- *IP.* Access to the VLE may also be limited using IP restriction, i.e. limiting VLE access to a range of known computers, probably located within the institutional library or IT labs. The IP is a unique numerical address on every computer. Only a few VLEs seem to provide this feature.

- *User roles.* Roles may typically be set at a system level and at the course level; system roles may include 'system administrator' (to manage the VLE hardware and software at the highest level) and 'non-administrator' or ordinary' user (to access the system interface only). Course-specific roles may include 'student' (to view documents and interact within communication tools) and 'course manager' (to update and manage an online course). Use of appropriate roles is an important security consideration, because higher level roles provide access to complex features, which if used improperly could damage the system or result in data loss (e.g. removal of user accounts).

- *Online course access.* Access to individual online courses will depend on registration in the relevant course, either achieved manually by an administrator, by a course manager (e.g. academic staff) or following self-registration by a student possessing a VLE account. The Blackboard system allows for self-registration using an 'access code' which is distinct from the user login, and allows users to access individual online courses. Once a user has self-registered on an online course, they need not self-register again on the same course, as the course may be accessed from the 'my courses' area. Self-registration may also be requested via e-mail sent directly from the VLE interface.

- *Group access.* Tutors may typically create custom group areas to allow collaboration among defined students on a particular online course. Group areas usually contain e-mail, discussion, chat or file exchange features. Group areas may also allow for e-mail list functions, allowing the tutor to e-mail a defined group from within the VLE. Although a student may be registered on a particular course, they will normally require rights from their tutor to access particular groups within the online course, allowing for private study groups.

- *Discussion board abuse.* It may be possible to limit or restrict abuse on discussion forums using moderation tools within the VLE; it may be necessary to disallow anonymous posts, or prevent the removal or editing of existing messages posted by students. Students may also be banned from groups or even given rights to manage discussion forums (useful for group area discussion).

- *Chat abuse.* Synchronous chat has traditionally been viewed as a problematic tool with regard to security, but modern VLE systems provide a range of features to ensure chat may be observed and moderated. Chat sessions may usually be recorded, providing a text record of all messages; additionally, some systems allow for the tutor to prevent users from typing in the message window unless given permission.

- *Online assessments.* Many VLEs provide online assessment tools, which may be used to provide online tests, either in the student's own time and venue (e.g. for distance learning) or within a controlled environment on campus (such as an IT lab). Methods to prevent cheating and other malpractices using assessment tools may include setting a defined timescale for users to attempt the test (e.g. between 9 a.m. and 10 a.m. on a particular date), hiding the test until the time of attempt, setting a password to take the test that is released at the time of attempt, or randomising the order of questions to deter copying from other computer monitors. Used collectively, these approaches may ensure online assessments are as secure as traditional tests, although this technology is of course in its infancy and should be used with caution.

Selling the VLE

The process of VLE deployment should include a range of stakeholders, including academic practitioners; similarly, the pilot stage of VLE deployment should involve student input to obtain first impressions and deal with obvious weaknesses.

User consultation and advocacy for the VLE should be two closely aligned objectives during early stages of deployment and staff should feel they have a voice in defining and developing the VLE service as a pedagogical tool. The general aim of the VLE should also be explained as integral to existing educational practice, i.e. a tool that may empower or facilitate current communications or course delivery, but not replace the pedagogy or educational role of staff.

Following an initial pilot or test, the working VLE should be presented to senior academic department leaders. This presentation should contain realistic scenarios to demonstrate core features, including:

- demonstration of online document publishing;
- demonstration of e-mail features to contact students or enable student queries;
- demonstration of discussion board features for topic-based debate;
- demonstration of group features for collaborative projects.

Early contact with academic departments may also allow for coordination of VLE development. Discussion should take place with departments to design templates for creation of online courses, including design of menu structures, use of department terminology and inclusion of subject-specific information resources.

The VLE should also be demonstrated to practitioners across academic departments, using structured training sessions to provide basic VLE familiarity and skills to manage online courses. Arrangements for setting 'course manager' rights should also occur at this point to provide course management access for tutors.

Although objections to the use of the VLE are inevitable, many staff will see the benefits of VLE use for communication and document-delivery purposes, particularly in supporting distance learning and part-time study. Care should be taken to explain VLE functions using realistic scenarios or examples during training, as this method will allow academic staff to empathise with VLE functions in the context of teaching activities.

Deployment of the VLE will necessitate a VLE strategy team or similar committee group; although VLE staff should have involvement in the development of VLE strategy, the strategy group should include both senior- and practitioner-level academic staff to ensure the strategy is appropriately informed by educational practice.

E-learning co-ordinators/champions

During the deployment of the VLE, some academic practitioners may demonstrate particular interest in using the system; such individuals may be appointed, either formally or informally, as a focal point for VLE development within their respective academic department or school.

Called variously VLE champions or e-learning champions, VLE leaders within academic areas should undertake appropriate training in the use of the VLE; this role will allow academic staff to approach an existing VLE practitioner for guidance on VLE issues and provide a contact for the VLE team to provide further training or support.

The role of support staff

Other institutional staff may be required to access and develop content on the institutional VLE; academic schools may employ secretarial or administrative staff to upload course content, manage user access or provide student support.

Support staff of this kind will require the same type of training extended to academic staff, but they may require only limited access to course management features (e.g. user management). In this case, a custom or alternative 'role' may be allocated, e.g. 'account administrator' or 'document manager'.

The following chapter will continue the theme of e-learning deployment as a managed project, considering the training requirements of e-learning users and approaches for training and user support.

4

Training and user support

Considerations

The climate in HE is rapidly changing, with growing financial challenges for students and increasingly market-driven skills demands; these influences, coupled with recent impetus for widening participation and increased co-operation with industry, have seen the emergence of a new user base within HE, characterised by increased diversity and changing study patterns.

The implications of this changing climate in HE include rising demands for core study skills and flexible approaches to support course delivery in a low-contact study context.

Recent legislation for accessibility has also defined the responsibilities of HE providers in delivering education for disabled users.

Although the use of VLEs and other forms of e-learning to support student–tutor interaction may be seen as a positive and innovative solution for facilitating low-contact and remote study, the impact of e-learning should also be seen in the context of challenges for students, tutors and other staff.

IT is becoming more prevalent in society, typified by home Internet access and growing ownership of PCs; however, it should not be assumed that all users will automatically possess IT literacy or familiarity with the Internet.

Although the following sections will relate more closely to training and support in the context of a VLE, many points will also apply to other forms of e-learning systems and applications.

Manual support

A range of methods should be used to support both the initial and the long-term use of e-learning systems for staff and students. Manual or person-to-person support for an e-learning system will typically include training sessions and incidental user support.

Policy and procedures document

At some point in the testing or pilot of an e-learning system, a practical 'policy and procedures' document should be developed to ensure service consistency and define service provision. This document should outline standard practices for activity on the system, including procedures for user training and support:

- procedures for creating and removing user accounts;
- procedures for allocating rights for advanced user access, e.g. 'course manager';
- procedures for the provision of support (i.e. methods for contacting support and standard approaches for recording and resolving queries);
- procedures for providing training (e.g. training structure, assessment methods);
- the role of individuals in providing training and user support (e.g. VLE staff, academic staff).

Training needs

The provision of quality and relevant user support is a crucial factor in ensuring system usability. Typically, there will be several audiences or user profiles for the provision of e-learning training and support:

- *E-learning system staff.* These individuals will comprise the core team for delivery of the e-learning system. The training needs of this group will reflect activity at the system and administrator level, including skills for technical and system management, and training of other institute staff.
- *Other e-learning support staff.* Incidental user support may be provided by other staff with an e-learning focus; the training needs of

this group will include the ability to perform defined activities on an e-learning system (e.g. user accounts administration) and process user enquiries.

- *Academic staff.* This group will use the e-learning system on a practitioner basis for student interaction and course delivery; the training needs of this group will include course management activities (e.g. document upload, communication tools) and pedagogical skills to facilitate learning and teaching via the e-learning system.

- *Academic support staff.* This group will provide support for academic practitioners in managing course content and some communication tools (e.g. notification for students via e-mail).

- *Students.* Student users will use the e-learning system to access online documents and interact with tutors and peers via a range of communication tools. The training needs of students may include basic web browsing skills and use of features within the e-learning system.

Filtered approach to training

Training may be passed on from system administrators who have undertaken formal training in a range of system functions to academic practitioners and other support staff; suitably trained academic staff may then provide training for students.

This filtered approach to training should ensure that each audience is provided with appropriate training for their level of system use, and should also provide a higher level of authority for each group to obtain support.

Delivering training

In early stages of system deployment, the emphasis will probably be on demonstrations for senior academic staff and other e-learning stakeholders; however, once pilot testing is complete and the system is deployed more widely, more formal training for practitioners and students should be provided.

The allocation of training provision should be appropriate for each user group or audience:

- *Administrators.* It is often advisable to obtain initial training for administrator-level staff from an authoritative third party, such as a VLE company or supplier. Administrators should receive training in all aspects of the system, including technical issues, system administration and use of the system front-end (e.g. online course management). Administrators will probably provide training to academic and student users, requiring this group to be fully familiar with the system.

- *Academic and other support staff.* This group will probably receive training directly from system administrators.

- *Students.* Students may receive training from administrators or suitably trained academic staff. In early stages of system deployment, it may be necessary to provide training entirely via system administrators; however, once academic staff are suitably familiar with the system, this group may be able to provide student training themselves.

A range of conventional methods may be used to deliver training for any of the above groups. The exact approach for training may depend on group size or the number of e-learning staff available to provide training. Most training sessions will include a demonstration component and practical 'hands-on' participation, involving use of networked computers to access the e-learning system:

- *Group sessions.* These could represent training for a few individuals or a whole department, combining demonstrations with hands-on practical examples.

- *One-to-one sessions.* A useful method for incidental training requests. This form of training will probably involve use of a networked computer for demonstrations and some practical examples.

- *Presentations.* An electronic whiteboard or projector may be used to demonstrate system features, either using a linear and explanatory approach (e.g. via PowerPoint presentation) or an actual system demonstration, illustrating key features via realistic practical scenarios.

- *Course-based training.* A formal and sequential format may be adopted for training sessions, introducing key system features across several planned sessions. Sessions may have demonstration, practical or written components. These sessions could contain an assessment component, with defined learning aims or objectives; VLE courses could also comprise a formally validated module within a staff or student induction programme. Obviously, this form of training should be implemented by suitably experienced or qualified staff.

New entry students (i.e. first-year students) should be provided with e-learning training within a normal induction process. Newly appointed staff should also be provided e-learning training as soon as possible to allow participation in e-learning activities within their department.

Although internal training may be provided by respective user groups, a range of external options exist for providing e-learning and other core IT training.

IT courses such as ECDL may be provided by an external provider or by internally accredited staff; e-learning-specific courses may also be provided, including courses for system administrators, academic staff or students. A range of IT training and related advisory services may be obtained from the following organisations:

- *Netskills* (*http://www.netskills.ac.uk*). Netskills provide a wide range of e-learning and general IT workshops, delivered across the UK at key venues. Netskills workshops can also be used to obtain Edexcel/BTEC qualifications in web development and e-learning. See the Netskills URL for the latest programme of events and courses.

- *Online Education and Training* (*http://www.ioe.ac.uk/english/ OET2.htm*). This course is based at the Institute of Education at the University of London, delivered either via distance learning (10 weeks) or combined online/class study (4 weeks). The course offers professional development for people who manage or support e-learning, including information service staff, IT-focused staff, educators and educational administrators. The course also provides useful preparation for research. The course is available in the UK and internationally. Additionally, the qualification can earn 20 credits towards either an Advanced Diploma in Professional Studies or a Master's degree.

- *Solent Training & Development* (*http://www.solentbiz.co.uk*). This company provides basic IT skills training and a range of e-learning courses.

- *Direct Learn* (*http://www.directlearn.co.uk*). A UK-based company, providing strategic advice and guidelines for use of e-learning systems.

- *Joint Information Systems Committee (JISC) RSCs – Regional Support Centres* (*http://www.jisc.ac.uk/index.cfm?name=rsc*). These JISC-funded support centres provide an advisory service for staff engaged in developing or deploying educational technology; this service is of most interest to e-learning developers or technical staff.

Although academic practitioners will have suitable teaching skills for student training, system administrator staff may not have teaching experience or formal teaching qualifications; owing to the large amount of student and staff training required by system administrators, these staff should undertake some form of teaching qualification, such as PGCE or similar accredited training.

Further training services are listed in Appendix 1.

Manuals, guidelines, etc.

Appropriate guidelines and manuals should be authored by qualified e-learning administrators for staff and student support.

Manuals, providing a detailed reference for the e-learning system, should be authored for students and academic users; manuals could also be made available to students during an induction process.

Shorter individual guidelines should also be made available on particular system features (e.g. downloading and printing files or using discussion tools); these guides could be made available in hardcopy format at an appropriate user service location (e.g. library enquiry desk).

Guidelines and related support documents may also be provided via an e-learning website or student intranet. Similarly, guides for staff may be made available via an e-learning area within the staff intranet, with a complete staff manual issued during system training.

Aspects to consider in authoring guidelines and similar documents may include:

- *Clarity.* Help documents should be written using a concise and uncomplicated style.

- *Avoid jargon.* It is often possible to replace some jargon or acronyms with plain language alternatives, e.g. URL becomes 'web address'.

- *Images.* Inclusion of screenshots may often demonstrate the process or actions required to carry out instructions.

- *Numerical stages or bullet points.* Separating an action or process into distinct logical stages, using numbers or bullet points, may assist users in carrying out otherwise complex actions or processes.

- *Provide further contact details.* Providing e-mail or telephone contact details may provide a useful reference for outstanding problems.

- *Frequently asked question (FAQ) format.* Use of a question-and-answer or FAQ-style document may provide an effective method for conveying lengthy instructions or otherwise complex information.

- *Realistic scenarios.* Description of typical learning activities within the context of support documentation may allow the user to empathise with system features.

For examples of good practice in authoring manuals and guides, see also Appendix 1 (VLE manuals and guides).

Other forms of user support

Incidental support may also be provided by trained support staff via an enquiry desk, telephone contact or during interaction with system administrators.

The e-learning or VLE 'policy and procedures' document should define procedures for managing incidental user support; which may include:

- students having forgotten login details to access an e-learning system;

- students requesting access to new online courses within a VLE;

- staff requesting further training using a particular system feature;

- students or staff reporting technical problems (e.g. error messages);

- students or staff experiencing web browser problems (e.g. JavaScript not working).

The provision of incidental user support via telephone, help-desk, etc., may include core e-learning staff or other information services personnel; the provision of e-learning support via traditional library-focused staff may require additional system training, including basic IT training (e.g. ECDL).

Automated and electronic support

User support may also be provided via automated or electronic means.

With increasing numbers of part-time and distance-learning students in a home study and online context, it is expected that students will wish to contact academic staff and system administrators using the convenience of e-mail.

Although most electronic support systems will involve use of e-mail, other online enquiry services may provide more sophisticated tracking and enquiry resolution facilities. A few common methods for electronic user support include:

- *Use of an e-learning website.* To provide a central location to access support manuals, guidelines, location details, opening hours and contact systems for specific forms of enquiry.

- *Provision of an e-mail address.* To contact system administrators – published on the e-learning website or other support literature.

- *Web-based feedback forms.* To allow students or staff to contact system administrators in a range of contexts, including staff training requests and general student enquiries.

- *Provision of e-mail within the e-learning system.* For students to contact academic staff.

- *Use of an automated enquiry system.* These types of system either use a web-based form or integrate with an existing e-mail address; once an enquiry has been made, the e-mail is logged and an enquiry confirmation is sent to the user's e-mail address. Once an enquiry is resolved, the enquiry status is modified appropriately. Automatic enquiry systems include the Virtual Reference Toolkit (*http://www2 .tutor.com/products/vrt.aspx*) and Trackit (*http://www.itsolutions .intuit.com*).

- *Use of interactive training.* Web-based interactive training may be authored using standard web editing software or may be provided within a VLE system using presentation features or Microsoft PowerPoint.

- *Microsoft Windows XP 'Remote Assistance'.* This Windows XP system feature allows technical support staff to log into a home computer with Internet access from a remote location as though they were using the home computer themselves. This feature allows the remote user to explore hardware or software problems and solve problems on the user's computer.

Academic staff

Training and support for academic practitioners will require an awareness of study context and the student profile of teaching groups.

It may be necessary to provide increased training for communication tools in a part-time or distance-learning context. Alternatively, training in content management may be more important in a blended or distributed learning context (i.e. combining class teaching with some use of e-learning).

Although academic staff will require training in the use of system features, pedagogical training in the use of e-learning should also be considered for academic practitioners. Academic staff may develop internal strategies and groups to facilitate best practice and share experience in using e-learning systems; external training may also be obtained for practitioners from a system developer or other authoritative company – see Appendix 1 (Pedagogy).

In addition to e-learning training and support, academic staff may require more general IT training, especially where staff are unfamiliar with core computing applications such as web browsers; in this case, provision of a general IT course such as for the ECDL may be required.

Similarly, academic practitioners should receive training in legal requirements, such as accessibility requirements for online course delivery and the impact of digital copyright and plagiarism (see Chapter 5 for further information on legal issues in the context of e-learning systems).

Students

Student training and support should be considered in the context of widening access, user diversity and an increase in low-contact study patterns.

The impact of the VLE and other e-learning software has provided a means to facilitate remote student–tutor communication and course delivery; students may now access course materials and interact with tutors from any location with Internet access. This 'ubiquitous' study approach has brought new challenges for student support.

With growing numbers of students registered on e-learning systems, academic practitioners may expect a dramatic rise in course enquiries via e-mail and other communication features; similarly, system developers and administrators may also receive large amounts of e-mail requesting technical or other support.

Perhaps the most important issue in dealing with incidental student support is the need for differentiation or filtering of enquiries using an appropriate process, to ensure enquiries reach the most appropriate authority or resource.

Access points to tutor contact details should be appropriately located, with system administrator details available on a general support website and specific academic support details within particular online courses.

Provision of access to a web-based support site may also solve a range of common user support problems, including login procedures, and printing and downloading files. Use of a 'questions-and-answer' or FAQ web page may also deal with common questions.

Care should also be taken to provide student training within the appropriate pedagogical context. It may be possible to provide a combined induction session using e-learning administrator staff to introduce system features, with academic staff demonstrating educational aspects. Alternatively, academic staff may acquire sufficient confidence to provide student training without e-learning administrator support.

Services for student training and incidental support should be designed to support a range of student profiles, including full-time, part-time, distance-learning and external students. It may also be necessary to write support literature with specific instructions for external users (where a special login or other non-standard procedures are required).

Role of academic support staff

Academic support staff include department administrators and other support staff providing auxiliary academic functions.

Academic support staff will require a range of e-learning training to facilitate tasks such as uploading course documents, adding and removing users on online courses or communicating with users via communication tools.

Although academic support staff will probably not provide student training, their role may provide a contact point for student enquiries (e.g. use of system features, communication tools). This category of staff should also be provided with guidance for directing students to other appropriate sources of information or support (e.g. academic staff for course items or VLE system administrators for technical problems).

Disabled users

Increased numbers of users possessing disabilities and other access problems have brought an added challenge for information services supporting the delivery of e-learning systems.

Although the provision of the e-learning interface as a usable and accessible medium should be the concern of system administrators, there is also a shared responsibility across the institute to ensure users with access problems may engage in learning activities in a fair and equal manner.

At the system level, administrators may assess an e-learning system to ensure compliance with industry-level standards (including accessibility standards).

Should the e-learning system conform to core technical standards such as XHTML 1.1 and also meet accessibility standards (e.g. WCAG), then we may assume a basic technical provision for accessibility has been met, allowing for a range of conventional or assistive software to view or read web-based systems.

Accessibility guides for users with access problems could be made available within information services access points (e.g. IT labs, accommodation halls); guides could also be made available in various colours, on audio tape, CD audio or VHS video to accommodate a range of accessibility preferences.

Documentation should also be made available dealing with technical accessibility issues such as web browser customisation (e.g. setting larger type sizes); guides may also be provided dealing with specific access issues within a particular e-learning system (e.g. how to change background or foreground colours).

The onus for accessibility support will lie partially with an e-learning team (e.g. in selecting/maintaining an accessible system), but liaison should also occur between qualified disability support staff and academic practitioners.

Specialist support may also be required to train disabled users in the use of third-party systems to access an e-learning system, including a Braille or screen reader for low-vision or blind users.

Chapter 5, Accessibility and legal issues, will consider the implications of access support in further detail.

Accessibility and legal issues

Overview

The deployment of an e-learning system or VLE is an integral component of institutional service provision. Front-end information systems should be seen in the context of legislation and industry-standard regulations, including copyright, data protection and accessibility regulations.

The rise of electronic systems to facilitate traditional information services has prompted legislation and sector-led recommendations to ensure system accessibility for users with disabilities and other access problems.

A recent survey by the Disability Rights Commission (2004b) has evaluated UK websites for accessibility; their report, *The Web: Access and Inclusion for Disabled People*, indicates significant non-compliance for web-based accessibility standards:

> ... most websites are inaccessible to many disabled people and fail to satisfy even the most basic standards for accessibility recommended by the World Wide Web Consortium. It is also clear that compliance with the technical guidelines and the use of automated tests are only the first steps towards accessibility ... (p. 5)

Access to electronic resources by users with access problems is clearly an important aspect for the design or selection of any front-end information system. Although the interface of the World Wide Web may appear a relatively simple and uncomplicated medium, both web-based and other Internet resources may present challenges for users with access problems.

Common disabilities and access problems include the following:

- *Blind or partially sighted.* These users will have problems accessing the textual and graphical medium of the Web.

- *Motor, mobility or dexterity.* This group may have difficulties inter-acting with more complex web features, such as forms, text boxes or buttons.

- *Cognitive.* This group includes users with learning difficulties; these users may prefer shorter, more concise navigation information or alternative briefer descriptions for longer text.

- *Colour blindness.* This group may have difficulties viewing certain combinations of colour (e.g. contrast of text colour against background colour). There are many forms and degrees of colour blindness.

- *Epilepsy.* The use of flashing objects or backgrounds on the Web or other Internet resources may trigger an epileptic seizure.

- *Deafness/hearing impairment.* Use of voice, sound or music in a digital context may present difficulties for deaf users.

- *Reading and writing.* Users with conditions affecting the ability to read, such as dyslexia or dyspraxia, may have difficulties interpreting complex web-based navigation or other descriptive information.

The presence of disability is widespread in the UK; according to the Royal National Institute for the Blind (2004), there are around two million people in the UK with a sight problem, with around half this number registered as blind.

A recent report by City University, London (2003) suggested that 4.6 per cent of HE students in the UK had declared a disability, with numbers expected to rise in the future.

Disabilities among the student population included:

- dyslexia: 1.68 per cent;

- deafness/hearing impairment: 0.30 per cent;

- mobility difficulties: 0.23 per cent;

- multiple disabilities: 0.32 per cent;

- blind/partially sighted: 0.15 per cent.

Typically, there are two basic layers or stages of information delivery via networked systems, the actual resource, delivered online via a networked system (server), and the access system (client) used to receive or access the resource.

Importantly, both the resource and the access system should comply with industry standards and accessibility legislation. For example, a resource such as a web document may be fully compliant with accessibility regulations, but the user may attempt to view this on a non-standard web browser which does not provide the latest accessibility support (e.g. to provide alternative text for images).

The process of publishing accessible resources may be considered as follows:

- The web resource, designed according to industry standards and accessibility guidelines, is provided online (e.g. via a VLE).

- The web resource is received by the disabled user, using software (e.g. a web browser) or other assistive technology compliant with industry standards, such as a screen reader to 'speak' the resource for blind users or a Braille reader to display text dynamically in the form of raised Braille characters.

Not all disabled users will require assistive technology to read or otherwise display web-based resources; many low-vision users will typically access the web via a standard web browser. Assuming both the web resource (e.g. web document) and the web browser (e.g. Internet Explorer) comply with industry standards, the user may customise the appearance of the web resource (e.g. font colour or size selection), or use other access features within the web browser (e.g. alternative text description of images).

Compliance with web standards should be seen as a standard model for delivering web-based resources in a universal rather than adaptive format. A web resource that conforms to industry standards and accessibility recommendations does not simply satisfy the law, but ensures resources may be accessed across the entire spectrum of standard web browser software, assistive technology and other software incorporating web browsing functionality.

Accessibility legislation

A range of legislation now defines the responsibilities of HE for the provision of accessible services. Although the emphasis of legislation is generic across a range of HE activities, these regulations also concern electronic and web-based services.

Disability Discrimination Act 1995 and amendments

(*http://www.hmso.gov.uk/acts/acts1995/1995050.htm*)

Originally passed in 1995, this Act defines the status of disability and describes the responsibilities of organisations to provide fair and equal provision for disabled users. Important aspects of this legislation include the following:

- A person is categorised as disabled 'if (they have) a physical or mental impairment which has a substantial and long term adverse effect on (their) ability to carry out normal day-to-day activities' (part 1.1).

- Employers are required to make 'reasonable' adjustment for employees having disabilities. This could include provision of assistive technology or special training.

- Since 1999, organisations are required to use 'reasonable adjustment' for disabled users in the provision of goods, facilities or services (including non-charging services); examples include 'access to and use of any place which members of the public are permitted to enter ...', 'access to and use of means of communication ...' and 'access to and use of information services'. The implications for HE clearly include provision of learner support services such as library or IT services and electronic learning resources.

- Organisations were required to provide a 'disability statement', outlining 'the provision of facilities for education and research made by the institution in respect of persons who are disabled persons ...' This statement may discuss the availability of electronic resources or provision for support in accessing these resources.

Further information on the Act may be obtained at Disability.gov (*http://www.disability.gov.uk/dda/*).

Additionally, an amendment to the Disability Discrimination Act (DDA) has been introduced for 1 October 2004, entitled *Rights of Access Goods, Facilities, Services and Premises*; this part of the DDA requires that services and facilities provide further 'reasonable adjustment' for disabled users, including physical aspects, such as building layout and general provision of services. The Disability Rights Commission (*http://www.drc-gb.org*) has issued guidelines for this amendment – importantly, web services are cited as examples of service provision:

An airline company provides a flight reservation and booking service to the public on its website. This is a provision of a service and is subject to the Act. (p. 13) (*http://www.drc-gb.org/open4all/law/code.asp*).

Special Educational Needs and Disabilities Act (SENDA) 2001

(*http://www.hmso.gov.uk/acts/acts2001/20010010.htm*)

This Act was passed in 2001 and requires FE and HE organisations to use 'reasonable adjustment' in delivering education for disabled users. Key aspects of the act include:

- The provision of services (e.g. library, financial services) for disabled users without 'substantial disadvantage in comparison with persons who are not disabled'.

- Institutions have a responsibility to provide 'anticipatory' adjustment for disabled students enrolling on courses, i.e. to prepare policy, procedures and resources, or employ personnel to support learning and teaching for disabled users as a standard feature of course delivery and not simply as a response to disabled applicants.

- A range of alternative formats are required for the provision of information, including hardcopy documents where electronic versions are not accessible or alternative colour schemes for colour-blind users.

- Reasonable adjustment is exempt where this will undermine academic standards, cause excessive financial difficulty, conflict with health and safety legislation or adversely affect the education of other students.

- Assistive technology should be provided where appropriate, e.g. screen readers, Braille readers.

- Support services should exist to support disabled users in the use of alternative access methods and assistive technology (e.g. disability support team).

- Electronic resources such as web pages, intranet sites and other digital resources should be accessible for disabled users.

Specifications for developing or auditing web-based resources for industry standards are discussed in the following pages (e.g. the W3C 'Web Content Accessibility Guidelines'); in the case of e-learning systems, case should be taken to research accessibility support before purchase, to ensure systems are compliant with industry standards.

Accessibility on the Web

Traditionally, the World Wide Web represented a range of proprietary technologies, with popular web browsers developing individual standards for the development of web content. However, in recent years, the World Wide Web Consortium (or W3C) has strengthened co-operation with software developers, accessibility organisations and other stakeholders to develop industry standards for the Web.

W3C (*http://www.w3c.org*) is the most influential standards-making body for the World Wide Web, chaired by the inventor of the Web, Tim Berners-Lee. This organisation develops the central technical standards upon which the World Wide Web relies.

Core standards developed by the W3C include the following:

- *CSS (cascading style sheets).* Traditional HTML (web documents) included tags to publish textual content (e.g. <P>hello</P> for paragraph) and tags to control colour and layout (e.g. <font color="black">). CSS are files which may be used to separate textual content from appearance, defining aspects such as text colour, size or layout; the use of the CSS file as an external control for document appearance means that accessibility systems may parse or understand web resources without the clutter of internal style tags.

- *HTML.* The basic standard or format for web pages is HTML, a file containing textual information enclosed by 'tags' that are used to display text, images or other multimedia using appropriate software, such as a web browser. Several versions of HTML have been defined, with the latest version named XHTML (extensible hypertext mark-up language). The main differences between traditional HTML and XHTML include the requirement for properly nested elements, lower-case tags and the need to close all elements (e.g. a correctly 'nested' paragraph which is also bold: <p><b>hello</b></p>).

  XHTML must also be well-formed (e.g. the purpose of <head> and <body> are more clearly defined); basically this means that XHTML is a stricter mark-up language than HTML. (For examples and tutorials, see the W3C schools site: *http://www.w3schools.com/xhtml/*

xhtml_html.asp). XHTML may also contain and interact with XML (extensible mark-up language), a purely descriptive language for use in web-based cataloguing and other descriptive purposes. There are several HTML-based mark-up standards defined by the W3C and supported by web browser software, including HTML 4.01 and XHTML 1.0. Although it is possible to use an earlier mark-up standard, the most recent standard is currently XHTML 1.1. Compliance with mark-up standards such as XHTML 1.1 will ensure web resources may be viewed or accessed by a range of software and systems, including standard web browsers such as Internet Explorer. For detailed information on mark-up standards, see Appendix 3.

- *WAI* (*Web Accessibility Initiative*). The WAI (*http://www.w3c .org/wai*) is a project led by the W3C to promote web accessibility and usability via the development of standards, use of guidelines, development of web authoring software and other promotional activities.

- *WCAG* (*Web Content Accessibility Guidelines*). The WAI has developed a set of 'Web Content Accessibility Guidelines' (*http:// www.w3.org/TR/WAI-WEBCONTENT*), which have become the industry standard for developing accessible web-based content. There are three levels of compliance within these guidelines: A (Priority 1 compliance) is the minimal level of compliance required, AA (Priority 1 and 2 compliance) provides increased accessibility and AAA (Priorities 1, 2 and 3) indicates the highest level of compliance. A range of automated tools may be used for testing WCAG compliance in web resources.

Another major standard for web resources are the US Section 508 Rehabilitation Act guidelines (*http://www.section508.gov*); although this standard is US-specific, the 508 guidelines are also based on the WCAG; the 508 accessibility standard is often listed in the specifications of web-based systems developed in the US.

Ensuring web resources contain valid mark-up and CSS is the first step in providing accessible web content; resources should also comply with the WCAG accessibility guidelines as far as possible, with an absolute minimum of level 1 compliance.

The above standards apply not only to traditional web pages, authored using manual systems such as Dreamweaver or FrontPage, but also to other web-based systems such as VLEs.

Assessing web-based resources

We have already considered web-based accessibility organisations, guidelines for accessibility and related legislation, but how can an e-learning system or VLE be assessed or audited for accessibility?

Initial consideration of web-based systems should involve some research into accessibility compliance. E-learning software developers may provide specifications defining accessibility standards support (e.g. AA or AAA). Other system providers may provide less detailed information, or may provide support for specific forms of disability or third-party systems.

Systems may be tested using automated software or web-based services; auditing web resources should be carried out using W3C-approved tools as far as possible. The following tools are some of the most useful:

- *W3C HTML Validator*. The W3C site provides a range of tools for checking the core standards compliance of HTML/XHTML web resources. Web resources containing HTML or XHTML errors may present problems for either standard web browsers or third-party equipment, such as screen readers. There are several validator tools available at the W3C site, including the W3C MarkUp Validation Service (*http://validator.w3.org*) and the Web Development Group Validator (*http://www.htmlhelp.com/tools/validator*), which also allows for multiple URL (web address) validation using a 'batch' option (this is also available as a Windows application – see 'A Real Validator': *http://arealvalidator.com/*).

- *W3C CSS Validator* (*http://jigsaw.w3.org/css-validator*). CSS used to control colours and layout may be checked using this tool. Checking style sheets is important to ensure standard CSS script is used for the layout of pages; pages may display incorrectly in standard web browsers if CSS errors or non-standard script is present. In some cases, use of non-standard CSS may result in unwanted effects within some browsers, including missing text, making web resources difficult to use.

- *Bobby*. This tool is available in the form of commercial software available from watchfire.com or using the free online version, limited to one validation per minute (*http://bobby.watchfire.com*). The Bobby system checks web resources for WCAG compliance, providing an appropriate logo to indicate the level of WCAG support. Bobby may be customised to check either the US 508 or WCAG standards. Bobby is one of the most widely used tools for WCAG auditing.

- *W3C logos.* Conformance with either of the three levels of WCAG accessibility also entitles developers to display the appropriate logo (A, AA or AAA). The W3C logos are available at *http://www.w3.org/WAI/WCAG1-Conformance.html*

Some VLEs cannot be assessed for accessibility using automatic tools and some manual checking for complex web-based systems will probably be required.

It should be noted that the above validation tools may be used for any web-based systems, including web pages developed manually using HTML editors (for details of web development software see Chapter 6).

Methods to ensure web accessibility and standards compliance include the following:

Note: To view HTML in Internet Explorer, first visit the URL of the resource you wish to check; click your *right* mouse button over the page, then select 'View Source' – a similar method is available in most other web browsers.

- *Use of TITLE.* The title tag is one of the most important tags in the HTML or XHTML document; this is used by a large number of web browsers to store a basic 'bookmark' about the web resource for later viewing. The title tag is also used by search engines such as Google and other systems for user searching and listing results, e.g.

  <title>University of Somewhere - Student Web Pages</title>

- *ALT tags.* Where images occur in web documents, an alternative textual description should be provided for non-visual users; this alternative text may be 'spoken' by a screen reader, e.g.

  <img src="pic.jpg" alt="A picture of John" />

- *Tables.* Tables in HTML should be defined using correct mark-up to indicate the presence of tabular data, and table headers (i.e. the row across the top) should contain a 'TH' tag to indicate the presence of a new column; tables used for layout should be avoided where possible. Additionally, a SUMMARY tag may be used to define the purpose of tables, e.g.

  <table summary="This table contains useful statistics">

- *Frames.* The web resource may consist of multiple windows (or frames) containing distinct web pages, such as a navigation window and 'main' display window. Frames should be avoided for accessibility compliance where possible, because they can disrupt or prevent access to web resources for some assistive technology. Significantly, the Blackboard system, which is the most widely used VLE, does use frames, although developers are beginning to develop non frames-based alternatives as accessibility standards and legislation become more prolific.

- *Interactive features.* Web forms, check boxes, drop-down menus and other interactive features may present difficulties for disabled users and assistive technology, such as screen readers. Interactive features (e.g. a selection menu) may often be replaced by simple hyperlinks. A range of methods exist to ensure interactive features are accessible, e.g. defining a 'tabindex' for easy selection of form options using the tab key on the keyboard, or 'access keys' to use web features without the need for a mouse.

- *Captions.* Similar to ALT tags for HTML documents, these consist of a textual alternative for more complex multimedia presentations, such as Macromedia Flash MX; typically, a caption will provide a short text description for audio or video files, which may be displayed on screen for users with hearing problems.

- *Alternative style sheets.* Several alternative CSS (style sheets) may be available within a web resource, allowing the user to select from a range of available styles to display the document, which could include a bold or larger font style. Not all current browsers support selection of alternative style sheets.

For detailed information on auditing HTML/XHTML, CSS and WCAG compliance, see Appendix 3.

A range of tools and automated services for auditing web resources are also available to download or use online, many which have become popular across the web development industry; however, it should not be forgotten that core standards such as XHTML, CSS and WCAG are the most important guidelines to observe for delivering both standards-compliant and accessible systems.

Accessibility tools for web authoring and validation of online resources include:

- *Accessible Web Publishing Wizard for Microsoft Office (http://cita .rehab.uiuc.edu/software/office/omp_welcome.html).* This plug-in provides a 'Save as accessible' option for Word, PowerPoint and other Office applications; the user is prompted to provide access information, such as alternative text for images. The resulting output is accessible HTML (though not necessarily WCAG compliant depending on the presentation content).

- *A-Prompt* (*http://aprompt.snow.utoronto.ca*). A Windows application for checking web resources for international standards, such as WCAG.

- *Betsie* (*http://betsie.sourceforge.net*). Not strictly a tool, but a system that may be run from a web server, allowing for a text-only view of web resources without having to provide a manually developed, non-graphical version of HTML pages. As the user follows hyperlinks, the pages are dynamically displayed in an accessible format. Betsie is provided by the BBC on a not-for-profit basis. This script requires some technical expertise to implement (i.e. CGI customisation).

- *Bobby* (*http://bobby.watchfire.com*). As seen in the online Bobby tool, this commercial Windows application is available for assessing WCAG or US 508 compliance.

- *LIFT for Dreamweaver/FrontPage* (*http://www.useablenet.com*). This plug-in provides detailed reports, interactive prompts and other features for developing accessible HTML/XHTML. There are two versions, one for FrontPage and another for Dreamweaver.

- *Patsie* (*http://www.tagish.co.uk/products/patsie*). An adaptation of the Betsie system for text-only web display, but provided commercially.

- *Text-transcoder* (*http://www.useablenet.com*). Another commercial text-only web display system.

- *Lynx* (*http://www.lynx.browser.org*). Not strictly an application; Lynx is a text-only web browser, and provides a useful tool for viewing web resources in a non-graphical format. Lynx is provided on a not-for-profit basis.

For further web authoring tools, see Chapter 6 and Appendix 1.

Although compliance with WCAG and other standards will assist disabled users in accessing web resources via the web browser, or using assistive technology, there is no guarantee that a compliant web resource may be used by every disabled user in the fullest capacity; for some disabled users, alternatives to electronic resources may be the most appropriate alternative, including hardcopy media or an assistant to provide support in accessing learning resources.

Delivering accessible systems

A range of software exists to facilitate access to web resources for disabled users; in many cases, ordinary web browsers may be used as an accessibility aid, where standard browser features may significantly enhance the user experience. Other specialist web browsers exist to provide added accessibility features (e.g. speech functions to 'speak' textual information).

Where a conventional web browser is not sufficient, third-party equipment may be required, such as a Braille display machine for blind users.

In addition to the above, the core operating system (such as Microsoft Windows XP) may provide useful tools for accessing digital or online resources:

Microsoft Internet Explorer 6

Internet Explorer allows the user to disable CSS (style sheets) provided with remotely accessed resources, and a custom style sheet may also be linked to the browser (e.g. provided by learning support staff) to set font colour, typeface, background colour and increased or decreased text size. 'Alternative text' for images may also be configured to display above actual images without the need to 'mouse-over'. A range of 'access keys' are also provided for users with motor or similar access problems, e.g. pressing the 'backspace' key takes the user back to the previous location (URL), whereas 'tab' moves to the next element on screen.

Netscape Navigator 7

Netscape provides a 'text zoom' feature to increase text size; fonts and colours may also be set within browser preferences. Netscape also supports selection of multiple style sheets if available within web resources; these may be selected using a basic pull-down menu. A range of keyboard shortcuts are also provided.

Opera 7

Opera provides a wide range of text customisation options, including preferences for setting minimum font size, colours and use of a custom style sheet to override remote resources. Font colours and size may also be set for particular HTML elements or objects, e.g. setting 'Heading 1' to a larger font size. Other features include left-handed mouse support and keyboard shortcuts.

Microsoft Windows XP

The XP operating system provides a range of accessibility tools, including a screen magnifier, an on-screen keyboard to access keys via an alternative input control (such as a joystick or mouse) and a narrator tool to 'speak' text-based documents. Other access features include 'sticky keys' to access Windows features using key combinations pressed incrementally; sounds may also be set to occur on Windows events. Additionally, Windows colours may be customised to provide high contrast and other colour schemes.

Screen readers

Screen readers such as JAWS and HAL provide web access for users with vision problems to 'speak' web resources. The latest version of JAWS provides support for a range of languages and integrates with the Internet Explorer web browser. (See Appendix 1 for URLs.)

Screen magnifiers

Most screen readers also provide screen or text magnification to increase the appearance of the screen display; accessibility software providing this functionality includes Supernova and Lunar.

Refreshable Braille readers

An option for users able to read Braille are refreshable Braille readers; these systems are third-party components that work alongside a typical computer, providing a dynamically generated Braille document (e.g. using raised pins beneath a flexible surface). Both HAL and Supernova support refreshable Braille displays. URLs for accessibility software are provided in Appendix 1.

Issues in assistive technology

Assistive technology may considerably enhance the experience of disabled users, but is unlikely to provide the fullest provision of services or information unless accessibility standards are strictly met and a simple, uncomplicated format is used for web output.

The ideal format for assistive technology is a predominantly text-based resource, containing minimal tables, images or special features.

It is also important to consider the arrangement of textual information in web resources, because assistive technology will usually 'read' the web resource in a linear fashion, i.e. from left to right/top to bottom; web elements used for complex layout, such as tables, may confuse assistive technology, misrepresenting the intended layout or sequence of information.

Additionally, accessibility also depends on standards compliance within the 'user agent' used to access resources (W3C 'User Agent Accessibility Guidelines' website 2004). The W3C has developed accessibility guidelines for web browsers and assistive technology (*http://www.w3.org/TR/UAAG10/*).

The W3C (2004b) has commented, in response the Disability Rights Commission Report (2004b), that this report fails to consider the compementary role of 'agents' used to access web resources, such as Braille readers, screen readers and web browsers, reccomending further development of standards for these systems:

> Essentially, the interpretation of the data in the report fails to account for the role of browser and media player accessibility, and the role of interoperability with assistive technologies, in ensuring that people with disabilities can use Web sites effectively.

Usability issues

Although accessibility is certainly an important aspect in the selection or development of a VLE or other web-based resources, web accessibility should be seen in the general context of usability and good practice.

Usability and accessibility are really complementary; usability may be informed by accessibility legislation, but also concerns interface design, clarity and the ability for users to interact with Web and other Internet systems without the need for substantial training.

Common features contributing to usability include the following.

Interface

The interface used to access web resources should be designed for ease of access, with a clearly defined navigation menu that provides a persistent route to areas within the resource (i.e. persistently on screen). Links within the interface should be defined using concise and relevant language (i.e. the name of menu items should relate to the content that will be accessed).

Navigation style

The navigation menu or links should consist of simple hyperlinks rather than complex script-generated buttons or roll-over images. Text rather than images should be used for interface navigation. Images or icons used to access information should be clearly defined, because the meaning of icons can be ambiguous.

Platform trends

Platform equipment includes the operating system used to run software, such as Microsoft Windows 98, Windows 2000 or Windows XP, the web browser used, e.g. Netscape Navigator 7, and the display resolution available to view web resources.

A controlled and standardised platform environment is possible on institutional computers e.g. providing Windows XP with Internet Explorer and a display with 1024 × 768 pixels resolution.

However, where home Internet access is required, it may be difficult to ensure a standard platform, because not all home users will possess standard computers capable of running the latest operating system or web browser. Although it is possible to issue guidelines for users accessing a VLE, e.g. based on supplier recommendations, care should be taken to ensure the VLE or other web resource is functional in a range of environments (e.g. non-Windows operating systems such as Apple Macintosh and a range of web browsers).

The W3C site provides detailed statistics on the kind of platforms used to access web resources. Currently, the most widely used web browser is Internet Explorer version 6 (with around 70 per cent using this browser), with other leading browsers including Internet Explorer 5, Opera 7 and Netscape variants. Consider this excerpt from the W3C site (2004):

Internet Explorer 6 is the dominating browser, XP is the most popular operating system, and most users are using a display with 800 × 600 pixels or more ... (*http://www.w3schools.com/browsers/browsers_stats.asp*)

CSS

These should be used to separate layout and other aspects of web appearance from actual content; where this is present in a VLE or other resource, assistive technology may parse or read textual information without the clutter of style code in the web document.

Custom style

A range of methods exist allowing users to modify the appearance of web resources. Some VLEs may provide a feature to increase or decrease text size or modify colours. Web browsers usually allow for modification of web content appearance by changing preferences within the application; Internet Explorer allows for a range of modifications, including the ability to disable resource-based style sheets and set custom text and background colour.

Alternative formats

Not all students will have appropriate software installed to view required document formats; for example, the Adobe Acrobat Reader application is required to view Acrobat Portable Document Format (PDF) files. If the student does not have the PDF viewer installed, instructions should be provided to download the appropriate viewer.

Similarly, not all disabled users will be able to 'read' proprietary file formats, such as PDF, Word, etc. Care should be taken to provide non-HTML-based files in an alternative format for disabled access, e.g. providing PDF in alternative HTML format. Software currently exists to provide websites or systems dynamically in an alternative text-only format, e.g. the Text Transcoder software from Usablenet.com. Care should also be taken to ensure automated format conversion software (e.g. text-only display) is compatible with more complex systems, such as a VLE.

It should be noted that assistive technology such as the JAWS screen reader does support some proprietary document formats such as Word and PDF. Additionally these formats also provide their own accessibility features such as 'zoom', alternative text for images and other inform-ative structural tags. (For information on accessibility features in Microsoft products see *http://www.microsoft.com/enable/* and for accessibility features in Adobe Acrobat (PDF files) see *http://www .adobe.com/enterprise/accessibility/main.html.*)

Bandwidth

Bandwidth is the capacity of a network to transfer data at particular speeds. All web pages and supporting files such as images must be downloaded into the user's client computer for viewing. The larger the file size (e.g. in kilobytes), the longer it takes to download. For academic institutions with high-speed Internet access, file size is not usually a problem, but Internet connection speed may be a problem for home users connecting to the Internet via a 56k modem.

Use of high-resolution images or content-rich documents such as Power-Point presentations should be carefully considered. For more details on bandwidth and reducing file size, see Chapter 3 (Publishing on the VLE).

Organisation of online resources

Resources on a web-based system or other Internet resource should be provided using a logical structure, reflecting organisational or course structures; for example, if a degree programme consists of a module proforma, a syllabus outline and an assessment schedule, this language should be used for linking to online resources.

Other examples include use of module names for folders containing module information or use of year names to represent levels of study.

Other legal considerations

As the VLE and other web-based resources comprise an integral part of institutional services, these electronic systems should comply with legislation in the same manner as traditional or manual forms of service delivery.

A range of legislation and regulatory organisations influence wider activities in HE, including the delivery of electronic resources.

Copyright, Designs and Patents Act 1988

(*http://www.hmso.gov.uk/acts/acts1988/Ukpga_19880048_en_1.htm*)

This is the most comprehensive Act defining copyright law, including original literary works, databases, musical works, artistic works, sound recordings, video and broadcast recordings. Reproduction of copyrighted material is restricted by permission of authors or other creators, unless permission is granted via an established clearance system licence. Works are protected by copyright regardless of the format or delivery mechanism used for display, including electronic methods.

Copyright for literary, dramatic, artistic or musical works expires 70 years after the author's death.

Copyright (Visually Impaired Persons) Act 2003

(*http://www.legislation.hmso.gov.uk/acts/acts2002/20020033.htm*)

This Act ensures that copying made in an accessible format for users with visual problems is not in breach of the 1988 Act, e.g. copying of a text resource to Braille output.

Copyright and Related Rights Regulations 2003

(*http://www.legislation.hmso.gov.uk/si/si2003/20032498.htm*)

This amendment to the 1988 act removes exception to copyright for research or private copying where this material will be used for commercial purposes.

CLA (Copyright Licensing Agency)

(*http://www.cla.co.uk*)

The CLA is the UK licensing body for reproduction rights, and is regulated by but is not part of the UK Government Patents Office; the organisation is non-profit-making and is owned by author and publisher groups. The CLA operates a range of fee-based licences for the reproduction of protected works.

The CLA HE photocopying licence allows for the reproduction of up to 5 per cent of most articles, book chapters, conference papers or individual poems, but does not include printed music, maps, private documents, bibles, liturgical works or newspapers. Currently, the HE photocopying licence applies to hardcopy reproduction only, i.e. paper-to-paper copying. Scanning and reproduction in other electronic formats require use of a separate transactional licence, allowing for the conversion of hardcopy documents to digital formats via OCR (optical character recognition). The HE photocopying licence is non-transactional, i.e. individual items may be reproduced under the 'blanket' licence without the need for an incidental fee, but scanning currently requires payment for individual instances of reproduction under the transactional licence.

Digital copyright

The CLA photocopying licence provides a 'blanket' or general entitlement to photocopy copyrighted materials; however the rise of e-learning systems has brought an increase in use and demand for electronic formats, often involving the process of scanning hardcopy documents to file formats such as Word or PDF.

In spring 2004, a new Digitisation Agreement was drafted between the CLA and HE institutions, outlining plans for the inclusion of document scanning and conversion to digital formats within the 'blanket' HE photocopying licence; this will effectively combine photocopying and scanning into a single licence.

Although the new licence has not yet been formally agreed, a range of proposals and issues are discussed:

- demands for a 'blanket' licence for scanning, allowing for internal regulation rather than use of a 'transactional clearance' scheme;
- the problem of US works outside the CLA remit;
- the problem of tracking or recording file distribution (individual downloads) within electronic systems such as VLEs.

Further information on digital copyright, including information on current and forthcoming licensing, may be found on the CLA website (*http://www.cla.co.uk/have_licence/he/he_digitisation.html*).

Other copyright clearance systems

The Newspaper Licensing Agency (NLA) represents the newspaper industry in a similar capacity to the CLA, providing licences for the reproduction of newspapers. Additionally, the Educational Recording Agency (ERA) provides licences for the recording of broadcast programmes for educational purposes, including films.

Other web copyright issues

Web-based resources are protected in the same manner as hardcopy resources under the 1988 Act; care should therefore be taken when quoting web resources (e.g. online articles).

Links to external web resources should also direct to the homepage of a distinct website, rather than linking to individual resources within sites; these kinds of external links should be appropriately labelled or described.

Copyright compliance within VLEs and other e-learning systems is certainly an important consideration when selecting or developing systems. Features should be available within systems to track or record the frequency of document downloads. Some systems, such as Blackboard, allow for the generation of reports demonstrating the frequency of document 'views'.

Methods should also be available to ensure copyrighted material published online may be easily registered with institutional clearance procedures.

Increased availability of quality scanning/OCR software and reliance on an electronic teaching context will undoubtedly ensure increased use of scanned materials; similarly, the increase of electronic journals and other online publishing may result in an increased use of digital formats within VLE systems.

Data Protection Act 1998

(*http://www.hmso.gov.uk/acts/acts1998/19980029.htm*)

This Act provides a responsibility for organisations to process information concerning private individuals in a standard manner. Personal information may include an individual's name, address, contact details or 'sensitive' information such as mental or physical condition, or religious beliefs. Eight principles are defined for the lawful storage and availability of data:

1. 'Personal data shall be processed fairly and lawfully ...' (in compliance with the Act).

2. 'Personal data shall be obtained only for one or more specified and lawful purposes, and shall not be further processed in any manner incompatible with that purpose or those purposes'.

3. 'Personal data shall be adequate, relevant and not excessive in relation to the purpose or purposes for which they are processed'.

4. 'Personal data shall be accurate and, where necessary, kept up to date'.

5. 'Personal data processed for any purpose or purposes shall not be kept for longer than is necessary for that purpose or those purposes'.

6. 'Personal data shall be processed in accordance with the rights of data subjects under this Act'.

7. 'Appropriate technical and organisational measures shall be taken against unauthorised or unlawful processing of personal data and against accidental loss or des-truction of, or damage to, personal data'.

8. 'Personal data shall not be transferred to a country or territory outside the European Economic Area unless that country or territory ensures an adequate level of protection for the rights and freedoms of data subjects in relation to the processing of personal data.' (Schedules Part 1 - The Principles).

Other responsibilities include:

- Responsibility to inform the Information Commissioner regarding information stored, including the individual subject(s), the form of information held and how data are used. (Part 3 17 - (1))

- Responsibility to provide access to information held on request, for no more than the maximum fee: 'A data controller is not obliged to supply any information under subsection (1) unless he has received (a) a request in writing, and (b) except in prescribed cases, such fee (not exceeding the prescribed maximum) as he may require.' (Part 2 - 7 - (2))

- Responsibility to cease using automated systems used for decision making on individuals if requested by the individual: '... in respect of which that individual is the data subject for the purpose of evaluating matters relating to him such as, for example, his performance at work, his creditworthiness, his reliability or his conduct.' (Part 2 - 12 - (1))

- Responsibility to clearly obtain permission for storing sensitive information such as race, ethnicity, religion, political opinions, union membership, health (physical or mental), sexual issues, criminal convictions or allegations. (Part 1 - 2)

Retention of personal data may occur within a VLE or may be provided via e-learning systems from a central data repository such as a student record system. Most institutions will have an internal data protection policy or procedures; use of personal data within electronic systems should comply with these internal arrangements.

Further guidance on the Act for public-sector bodies, including fees, may be obtained from the Information Commissioner's Office website (*http://www.informationcommissioner.gov.uk/eventual.aspx?id=87*).

Welsh Language Act 1993 (including general language issues)

(*http://www.legislation.hmso.gov.uk/acts/acts1993/Ukpga_19930038_en_1.htm*)

This Act, pertaining to Wales, created a Welsh language board to oversee a range of regulations relating to the provision of 'public business and the administration of justice' for the Welsh language.

Public bodies, such as local authorities, schools and universities, were required to hold 'schemes' that outline institutional policy or procedures to facilitate services and other public information in the Welsh language 'so far as is both appropriate in the circumstances and reasonably practical' (Part 2), and that 'the English and Welsh languages should be treated on a basis of equality' (Part 1).

See the following pages for issues on provision of e-learning systems for multiple languages.

General language issues

Support for a multilingual context is growing among many VLE systems; the main issue surrounding multilingual support within VLEs is the system interface or front-end, providing menus, hyperlinks and other navigation to access system features.

There are two basic approaches to customising the VLE interface for customised language support. One option is to modify the textual buttons and navigation of the VLE to reflect a particular language, and this will usually replace existing text in the original language (probably English); only limited customisation may be possible using this method, as some interface features may be 'locked' or non-customisable. Additionally, modification of interface text may provide a means to display an alternative language, but does not solve the problem of supporting several languages, where users require the ability to customise the interface language.

A second option, available in some VLEs such as Blackboard ML and WebCT Vista, is the availability of pre-made language packs installed within the VLE, providing the option for users to choose their required language within the VLE interface. Currently, no VLE yet provides particular support for the Welsh language, although much debate has occurred between VLE clients and software developers on this issue. Additionally, some open source systems would, in theory, allow for participation in development of system text to reflect a desired language.

Although customisation of the VLE interface to reflect particular languages is a major issue for multilingual display, another related issue concerns multilingual content. The availability of translation expertise is usually a resource problem in delivering multilingual documents. Additionally, the use of external websites (which are constantly updated by their owners) will be impossible to provide in other languages.

One solution for content translation is the use of automatic online translation systems, used to display web resources in a range of languages. Translation occurs dynamically on all content viewed, preserving hyperlinks and other features. Although these systems provide an efficient method for online translation, the automatic translation output is not always perfect, with some semantic and grammatical errors.

Automatic translators include Babelfish (*http://www.babelfish.com*) and Translation Experts (*http://www.tranexp.com*), which also supports Welsh. Translation systems may not function with some VLEs and other complex web systems, owing to a lack of authentication support, so may only be suitable for conventional websites. In addition, output may not comply with the Welsh Language Act.

Support for languages such as Welsh is certainly growing among VLE developers. The Windows XP operating system and Office 2003 will also be available in the Welsh language (*http://www.microsoft.com/resources/government/LocalLanguage.aspx*).

Other online learning tools

Overview

The VLE model is becoming a popular approach for the delivery of e-learning, providing a wide range of content publishing, communication and online assessment features; however, a wide range of specialist applications and systems are also available for web publishing and other educational support in an online context.

The most widely used software supporting the delivery of e-learning is probably the Microsoft Office suite. The Office suite is used by teaching practitioners to publish textual documents, presentations and spreadsheets, with students often required to submit coursework in Office formats. Additionally, the Office suite integrates with most web browsers, providing seamless access to Office documents via the web interface.

However, the Office suite is also a commercial application, and by its nature does not guarantee universal ownership or availability for institute users. Additionally, disabled users may be unable to view some file formats, such as Word, PowerPoint, etc., using screen readers or other assistive technology.

Alternative methods of resource authoring include conversion of proprietary formats such as PowerPoint into an HTML presentation, which may be viewed on any web browser, or use of applications for the creation of learning resources compatible with international standards, such as Instructional Management System, which can be uploaded into a range of e-learning systems.

The authoring and compilation of resources for delivery via the Web or e-learning systems is a complex issue, demanding consideration for the usability, accessibility and availability of resource formats. Care should also be taken to ensure resources provide the practical functionality required by users in a particular learning context, e.g. a

Word file may be viewed, printed, saved from the Web or edited; however, the ability to view this format depends on availability of the Word helper application.

Scanning and OCR

Document scanning describes the method of creating a digital text resource from a hardcopy (printed) source. Importantly, the resulting file is not simply an image or photograph of the document, but comprises a text document, composed of characters.

The 'flatbed' scanner is the most popular form of scanning equipment on the market, comprising a space-efficient desktop appliance allowing scanning from A3 size to smaller dimensions. The usual process of scanning is summarised as follows:

1. A hardcopy document is laid on the glass pattern of the scanner, and the scanner software is then 'run' by the user (e.g. software provided with the scanner).

2. The user selects an output format for the scanned file, e.g. an image file such as JPEG or text format such as '.txt' (ASCII).

3. Once the scanning is complete, the file may be saved to the user's hard disk.

4. If a text format was specified, the scan may be converted to text using OCR software.

Scanning is also possible using tools provided with the Windows XP operating system and other versions of Windows (e.g. Control Panel/Scanners and Cameras). Additionally, printed documents may be scanned directly into third-party applications, such as Word or Acrobat.

Traditionally, scanning was an expensive and time-consuming activity, but cost-effective scanning equipment and sophisticated software now allow for a relatively easy process. Some common applications used for scanning include the following:

- *Microsoft Office XP* (*http://office.microsoft.com*). The Microsoft Office suite of applications include scanning integration, providing the ability to 'insert' text or other content from the scanner directly into Word, PowerPoint and other applications; this allows for the creation of Word documents (and other Office files) directly from printed documents.

- *Adobe Acrobat PDF* (*http://www.acrobat.com*). The Adobe Acrobat application (commercial version) allows for the creation of PDF (portable document format) files, containing text or multimedia. PDF files may be viewed using the free Adobe Acrobat Reader. The main advantage of the Acrobat format is its low file size, allowing for faster downloading. Acrobat documents (PDF) may be created directly from the scanner, using OCR to create a text-based document.

There are obvious copyright issues surrounding scanning and distribution of converted documents; care should be taken to ensure scanning of published articles or other copyrighted documents is undertaken within institutional regulations and copyright clearance procedures (e.g. CLA). For further details of copyright law, see Chapter 5.

Document authoring

We have already noted several approaches to document authoring, including use of Office applications, such as Word and Acrobat for PDF documents.

At this point, it may be useful to consider two basic forms of document format or delivery mechanism for web publishing: application-based formats and HTML format:

- *Application-based formats.* Document formats such as Word or Acrobat often allow for more precise and sophisticated text editing, but rely on the use of a respective application for authoring and viewing via the web browser. The web browser itself only understands simple text-based files based on the ASCII format; more complex document types (Word, PowerPoint, Access, Acrobat, etc.) typically use machine readable (binary) content and cannot be viewed in web browsers without the correct 'helper' application.

- *HTML format.* HTML-based files (web pages) may be viewed directly in the web browser without the need for additional helper applications. This is because web browsers understand the simple ASCII text format used to create HTML files and the HTML tags used to present marked-up content.

Each of these approaches to document publishing has subtle advantages and disadvantages.

Application-based formats (Microsoft Office applications etc.)

- Such formats provide more precise document editing than plain text/HTML format.

- Such formats provide integration of text and supporting files (e.g. images) within a single integrated file (e.g. a Word file or .doc).

- Such formats are portable and reusable, i.e. relatively easy to view, download, print, save or distribute

- Documents may be edited or manipulated following download, assuming the appropriate helper application is available (with the exception of Adobe Acrobat PDF documents, which are less easily modified, but can usually be converted to a simple plain text format).

- Care should be taken to ensure students are suitably aware of appropriate viewers (e.g. viewers for Office formats, Acrobat Reader).

- Support for application-based documents with assistive technology such as JAWS is improving but author knowledge of accessibility features in the relevant application is essential.

HTML format

- The format is not always easily portable, because supporting files (e.g. images, CSS) remain outside the HTML document.

- HTML may be viewed in any standard web browser, removing the need for 'helper' applications.

- Use of HTML format as a second option for viewing is often a good idea when using a proprietary format for web publishing, such as Word.

- It may be possible to upload HTML-based documents with supporting files (such as images) within a VLE, usually in the form of a zip archive – see the next section for details of using HTML within a VLE.

- HTML files are simpler than application files (ASCII text based as opposed to binary etc.) and are generally more accessible.

Although HTML-based approaches are discussed in the next section, it may be worth considering a few application-based formats:

- *Microsoft Office (http://office.microsoft.com).* The Office suite includes Word (word processor), Excel (spreadsheet program) and Access (database program); the FrontPage HTML editor is also included (see next section). Although the primary output of Office files is application dependent (e.g. Word 'doc' files), the Office applications also have the ability to 'Save as Web Page', allowing for the creation of HTML documents, which may be viewed via the web browser without the need for the relevant Office application.

- *Microsoft accessories.* Often forgotten, there are several basic applications bundled with the Windows Operating System, including Microsoft Notepad, which allows for the creation of basic (ASCII) text files, and Microsoft WordPad, which allows for the creation of rich text format (RTF) files, a fairly powerful word processing standard that is viewable on most operating systems.

- *Open Office (http://www.openoffice.org).* This is an 'open source' and not-for-profit alternative to the Microsoft Office suite of applications, including database, presentation, word-processing and other applications. Open Office provides similar functionality and is compatible with Microsoft Office programs such as Word; support is also provided to create Acrobat PDF documents without the need to purchase the commercial Adobe Acrobat software. Multiple languages are also supported, including a Welsh version under development.

- *Star Office (http://wwws.sun.com/software/star/staroffice).* The Star Office suite, developed by Sun Microsystems, is based on Open Office and is also compatible with Microsoft Office applications. Features include a PDF export option and support for assistive technology. Star Office provides a free licence for educational organisations, but is otherwise a commercial application. Use for educational staff or students outside the place of study is possible using a special distribution agreement with the Sun company.

Web authoring (HTML based)

In some contexts, it may be more appropriate to provide resources using an application-based format, such as Word; this may be required for document portability, i.e. the ability for users to download, edit and store files on a personal computer.

Suitably trained or experienced staff may be able to create resources using HTML editors; these applications often provide a word processor style editor to create either stand-alone web pages or entire websites. Basic understanding of HTML is usually necessary for the creation of HTML-based resources.

Although it is beyond the capacity of this book to describe fully the possibilities of HTML authoring, key features include:

- *Hyperlinks.* As discussed in Chapter 1, hyperlinks provide a method to link to other web pages or resources, including external websites on the World Wide Web, e.g. <a href="http://www.w3c.org">The W3C Site</a>.

- *Multimedia.* It is possible to display a range of supporting files in HTML documents, including images (e.g. JPEG, GIF), digital sound files (e.g. MIDI) or digital video (e.g. MPEG). Consideration for file size and bandwidth is important in using supporting multimedia files; the HTML document usually comprises only a minimal file size, although supporting files such as images may be much larger.

- *Interactive features.* These include feedback forms, guestbooks and other interactive features; these kinds of features are included within most VLEs. However, development of stand-alone interactive features within traditional websites hosted on a web server will require some expertise in advanced web technology such as Perl or ASP.

It is advisable that staff wishing to use web authoring software should attend some kind of course on web development basics, such as a City and Guilds or BTEC qualification. A useful introduction to HTML is also available on the W3C 'schools' site (*http://www.w3schools.com/html*).

Web authoring tools

The following web development software may be used to create HTML for a conventional web server (e.g. a stand-alone website), and may also be used to create documents for uploading within a VLE.

To upload a number of linked web pages, these may often be combined in a zip archive, using the WinZip application (*http://www.winzip.com*). This application allows for merging all HTML and supporting files into a single compressed file with a .zip extension, e.g. 'myweb.zip'. This zip file may then be uploaded to the VLE according to system instructions. Otherwise, single HTML files may be uploaded to the VLE without use of WinZip, although this basic method may not support linked files such as images (it is also possible to create/unpack zip archives in Windows XP without Winzip installed).

Web editing software for stand-alone use, or use within VLEs, includes:

- *Amaya (http://www.w3.org/amaya).* This combined web editor and web browser provides a word processor style interface, allowing for easy creation of HTML or XHTML documents. The main feature of Amaya is the ability to browse to a web address (via the Amaya web browser) and actually edit the web page 'on the fly' (assuming login rights are set). Amaya is available on a not-for-profit basis.

- *Microsoft FrontPage (http://office.microsoft.com).* This commercial web editor is available separately or as part of the Microsoft Office suite. FrontPage provides a simple word processor style interface and also allows for the creation of a 'FrontPage Web', linked to a FrontPage web server, providing authors with the ability to create and manage HTML/XHTML documents entirely within the FrontPage interface. Because of its simplicity, FrontPage is the ideal entry-level web editor for new web developers.

- *Macromedia Dreamweaver MX (http://www.macromedia.com).* This commercial web editor is similar to FrontPage, but provides a rather different interface and more powerful features, including fuller integration with advanced web technologies such as Flash and ASP. Dreamweaver provides access to a local or remote server for HTML authoring, via FTP or local area network file access. A range of Macromedia plug-ins and extensions may be added to Dreamweaver to create educational web pages, such as sequential learning resources. One of the main strengths of Dreamweaver is the ability to create 'template'-based sites, which may allow for shared access to web content, but restrict control over certain parts of the web page, such as menus, headers or style.

- *Macromedia Contribute (http://www.macromedia.com).* This commercial software presents a similar but simpler interface than Dreamweaver MX, intended for a wider, non-technical audience. A template system ensures users are able to modify only existing pages that have been created, or prevent inclusion of certain content within web pages; this system also includes the ability to 'drag and drop' Word files into the editor for immediate conversion to web pages.

- *Macromedia e-learning Suite 2004 (http://www.macromedia.com).* This package of Macromedia applications includes Authorware, Flash MX and Dreamweaver MX.

- *Netscape Composer (http://www.netscape.com).* This web editor is similar to FrontPage, but is provided free with the Netscape Navigator web browser. This is another simple, entry-level web editor.

Although the creation of HTML-based resources for the Web or use in VLEs may appear an attractive method of content authoring, steps should also be taken to ensure staff using web development tools are suitably trained and are familiar with basic web usability and accessibility issues. Quality assurance procedures should be in place to ensure HTML content conforms to accessibility standards; this could involve a content submission process in which suitably skilled staff could check HTML resources using accessibility tools such as Bobby (further quality assurance issues are discussed in Chapter 7).

Web-based multimedia

A range of audio and visual file formats may be created for use in a web context. At the simplest level, video and sound files may be provided via a simple hyperlink within a traditional web page, or may be uploaded within a VLE to allow user downloading and playback. Audio and video files may be included within presentation software, such as PowerPoint, to create a complete presentation, incorporating sound, audio, text or other content for publishing via the Web or VLE.

Creating audio and video files

When creating or using audio or visual files, it is important to use an appropriate file format. File size and bandwidth limitations may restrict the ability of home users on slow modem Internet connections to download large multimedia files, so care should be taken to ensure web-based multimedia files are as efficient as possible in relation to file size and actual duration (playing time).

Note that audio and video files may be created using various levels of compression within respective multimedia creation software, usually providing the ability to create higher quality multimedia or lower quality files; the higher the quality of the output file, the more disk space and longer downloading time is required. Conversely, compression of multimedia files to save disk space and reduce download time usually results in some loss of quality.

Many of the following multimedia file formats may be expected to play using standard Microsoft Windows software (i.e. Windows Media Player) and similar software on other operating systems (such as Linux); however, a few formats require a special plug-in or codec, which may be downloaded separately.

Common multimedia file formats include:

- *WAV.* This audio format provides a high-quality output and is compatible with a wide range of operating systems, usually without the need for additional plug-ins.

- *MIDI.* This audio format produces an output of efficient file size and will work on most systems without the need for additional plug-ins.

- *AU.* Another audio file supported by Windows.

- *MPEG Audio.* This audio format allows for significant file size compression and should work on any Windows system without additional plug-ins.

- *MP3.* This audio format provides very high levels of file size compression while retaining high-quality output and is becoming one of the most popular formats for publishing sound files. MP3 audio is now supported by Windows Media Player.

- *MOV.* This is the QuickTime video format, which is widely used but requires the QuickTime codec to run.

- *AVI.* This is a common video format providing good levels of file size compression and support via standard operating systems (e.g. Windows Media Player).

- *MPEG Video.* Another video format providing high levels of compression and supported by Windows Media Player.

- *DIVX.* This video format provides very high levels of compression while retaining video quality. DIVX video usually requires an additional codec available from the DIVX development website (*http://www.divx.com*).

Audio and video files may be created using a range of applications, including basic software provided with the Windows operating system; however, appropriate equipment will be required to create multimedia files using appropriate software. A few input devices used to create video and sound include:

- *Microphone.* A standard microphone may be connected directly to the PC 'line-in' audio socket, and may be used to record speech, music or other audio using appropriate software, such as Windows Sound Recorder.

- *Other audio input.* Other audio sources may be connected to the PC for digital sound recording, including audio cassette and audio CD.

- *Web cam.* A web cam is a digital camera that may be used to record either still images or provide video recording for the creation of digital video files (e.g. using Windows Movie Maker), or transmission of video in real-time over the Internet for video-conferencing-style communication (e.g. using Microsoft Net Meeting).

- *VHS video source.* VHS video may be imported for creation of digital video files using a special 'video capture' device installed on the computer. This is often useful to preserve older VHS films, documentaries or other filmic material.

A range of audio and video applications are available for the creation of sound and video files:

- *Microsoft Sound Recorder.* This application is provided with the Windows operating system, allowing for the recording of WAV format files; several quality levels are available for reducing file size, although WAV files may later be compressed or converted to other more efficient formats such as MPEG or MP3 using an audio editor such as Goldwave (*http://www.goldwave.com*).

- *Microsoft Movie Maker.* This application may be used with a webcam or other digital video recorder to record digital video files directly on the PC (e.g. MPEG format). Movie maker may also be used with video capture hardware on a PC to convert VHS or other legacy video formats (i.e. non-digital sources) to digital formats. Existing digital video files (e.g. MPEG) may also be loaded into Movie Maker for editing or 'cutting' individual frames.

- *Audio editing.* Audio files may be edited (e.g. by removing or adding audio content), 'resampled' (i.e. compressed) or converted to other formats (e.g. from WAV to the compact MP3 format). A popular commercial audio editor is Goldwave (*http://www.goldwave.com*).

- *Audio streaming and RealAudio.* Another option for creating and publishing audio is the use of streaming, in which small packets or chunks of audio data are delivered sequentially, and played when packets are received. Additionally, a 'buffering' method is used to play received audio data a few seconds after actually receiving the stream. This method effectively allows for playing audio from the web browser without the need for a long single download. This method may also be used to protect the actual audio source, because the user is not actually downloading the entire file. The RealAudio format (*http://www.real.com*) is the most common streaming application, requiring a RealAudio streaming server and availability of the RealAudio application on the user's machine. The requirement of a RealAudio server is probably the only major drawback for use of this approach.

Using audio and video files

Once audio or video files have been created, they may be simply uploaded within a VLE and provided via a basic hyperlink for user download; in some cases, options may be available to display audio or video files within the VLE with sound controls to 'play' the resource.

In most cases, multimedia files will open seamlessly from the web browser, usually invoking an appropriate application within the operating system, such as Windows Media Player; however, in the case of DIVX, MOV and other proprietary formats, instructions should be provided for downloading the appropriate viewer or codec.

Before publishing an audio or video file online, care should be taken to ensure the file size of the resource will not pose a problem for users; if the file size is several megabytes, the file may take a long while to download for home modem users. For larger files, compression using a multimedia editor, such as the Goldwave audio editor, should be considered. Compression may also be possible using a presentation tool (see next section).

Presentations

There are various approaches to publishing presentation-style resources via traditional web pages or a VLE. Presentations typically comprise multiple slides or frames, containing text, images and other multimedia, which may be viewed sequentially. Presentations may also provide navigation menus to view particular stages of a presentation sequence, or may provide other interactive features, such as a self-assessment for testing understanding of viewed material.

Applications such as PowerPoint allow for the creation of a single file, containing text, images and other multimedia files, which must be viewed using the PowerPoint application installed on the user's computer or a compatible viewer (e.g. the free Microsoft PowerPoint viewer).

Presentations may also be created using HTML-based tools, providing text, images and multimedia as an HTML-based resource, which may be viewed directly in the web browser without the need for helper applications.

- *PowerPoint (http://www.microsoft.com)*. PowerPoint is probably the most popular application for authoring and publishing presentations. PowerPoint allows for a wide range of media types within the presentation, including digital video and special features such as slide transitions. PowerPoint presentations are primarily saved in the .ppt format, which requires the PowerPoint application or viewer, but files may also be saved and published in an HTML format.

- *Producer for PowerPoint (http://www.microsoft.com/windows/ windowsmedia/technologies/producer.aspx)*. Microsoft Producer is a free extension for PowerPoint, allowing for the creation of web-based presentations containing digital video and PowerPoint files; PowerPoint slides may be synchronised or timed to display with digital video clips; the final presentation may also be set to auto-run. Producer requires a little training for most users, but the authoring process is relatively easy and the output is simple. This tool provides an excellent method of creating reusable resources involving dictation or speech (e.g. lecture presentations). Producer also compresses files for faster downloading. *Note*: You should consult the Producer website to ensure your version of PowerPoint is compatible.

- *Impatica for PowerPoint or Director (http://www.impatica.com)*. Impatica allows for the conversion of PowerPoint or Director presentations, containing images, audio or video files, into a compressed Impatica format (.imp). This compressed file may be uploaded into the Impatica OnCue application, alongside additional digital video, to create an HTML-based presentation. The main feature of Impatica is its ability to shrink typically large presentations into smaller files for publishing via the Web or VLE; images and multimedia files will all be radically compressed, allowing for much faster downloading.

- *Boxmind Flashpoint* (*http://www.boxmind.com/products/flashpoint*). This application converts PowerPoint files into a compressed Java format for publishing on the Web. The resulting presentation should download faster than the original PowerPoint file, and may be viewed on any web browser with Java support.

- *Macromedia Flash MX* (*http://www.macromedia.com*). The Flash application may be used to create graphical presentations using images, multimedia files, vectors (lines, colour, fill, etc.) and text. A drag-and-drop interface is available, allowing for the creation of animations, which may also provide user interaction (e.g. menus, option selections). The resulting SWF file may be used in a range of contexts, including HTML files. The free Macromedia Flash player is required for viewing Flash files in the web browser. The use of Flash MX requires appropriate training.

- *Macromedia Director* (*http://www.macromedia.com/director*). Another multimedia tool allowing for animation and interactive features; the output files created by Director are called 'Shockwave' and require the free Shockwave plug-in to function on a viewer's browser.

Assessments

Most VLE systems such as Blackboard and WebCT provide a fully featured, internal assessment system, allowing for the creation of online tests using a range of question types, such as 'fill in the blank', 'multiple choice' or 'matching' questions. Points or scores may be allocated to individual questions and students may attempt assessments online from any remote location via the VLE. Assessment results are usually recorded automatically within an internal spreadsheet feature, although some manual 'marking' may be required for open-ended 'essay' questions; statistical reports are also usually available.

Additionally, VLE assessments usually provide security features to minimise copying and other forms of malpractice, such as password protection or time limit features for assessment completion.

Alternatives to assessment systems within VLEs such as Blackboard, WebCT and Bodington usually involve a similar online context, automatic marking and similar question formats (multiple choice etc.). Most of the following assessment systems require server hosting, i.e. installation of the assessment software on an institutional web server:

- *Questionmark Perception (http://www.questionmark.com).* Question-mark provides a range of assessment tools, including Perception for Windows and Perception for Web; in the web version, assessments may be authored online via the web browser and made available online for student completion. The Perception for Windows version provides a Windows desktop interface (non-web based). Perception includes automatic marking and report features.

- *Granada Testwise (http://www.learnwise.com).* This software forms part of the Granada Learnwise VLE or may be purchased separately as a stand-alone service. A range of question formats are available, including automatic marking, reporting and analysis features.

- *Teknical E-Learning Questions (http://www.teknical.com/Products/ elearning_questions.htm).* This assessment feature is provided with the Teknical Virtual Campus VLE or as a stand-alone product. Assessments are created using a Windows-based application and may be uploaded into compatible e-learning systems. A range of multimedia formats may be included with assessment questions.

Collaboration and online conferencing

VLE systems provide a range of communication and interactive tools for collaboration and exchange of information, including real-time chat, use of electronic whiteboard, e-mail, discussion features and document submission.

Other systems providing similar online communicating include the following:

- *Microsoft Exchange (http://www.microsoft.com/exchange).* This server-based system provides users with a collaboration system similar to the Microsoft Outlook e-mail and calendaring application. Exchange provides shared calendars, shared address books, e-mail and other collaboration tools. The exchange user typically accesses an exchange account via a web interface or the Exchange desktop application.

- *Colloquia (http://www.colloquia.net).* This relatively simple application provides group-based communication via discussion, file exchange and distribution of online learning resources according to IMS and SCORM standards (defined below). Colloquia is not a content publishing system and does not 'serve' web content or require a server system. Colloquia requires only that each user installs the Colloquia application on their home computer. All communication via group discussion, file sharing, etc., is achieved using e-mail technology. Colloquia is also available on a not-for-profit basis for educational organisations.

- *Microsoft NetMeeting.* NetMeeting is available at *http://www .microsoft.com/windows/netmeeting* (check site for compatibility with your system) and provides real-time chat, file transfer, interactive whiteboard and file sharing; NetMeeting also provides face-to-face video conferencing using a webcam or other video source and real-time audio communication.

- *Windows Messenger.* Messenger allows for sending instant messages to other Windows users, audio, video communication, file exchange, text-based chat and integration with 'remote assistance' to allow remote login to the local PC by a technical support service. Messenger is provided with most versions of Microsoft Windows.

- *ICQ (http://web.icq.com).* This application provides similar functionality to Windows Messenger and may also be used via a web browser interface at the ICQ website. ICQ is a world-wide chat system, and should be used with care in any serious context.

Learning objects and VLEs

Background to learning objects

Early VLEs were proprietary, allowing for uploading and management of content without the capability to migrate materials to other systems easily.

More recently, standards have been developed for the creation of web-based educational resources, including sequential learning presentations and interactive assessments. These learning objects are intended for viewing via a web browser using intermediary web-based software such as a VLE or a compatible 'viewer' such as a Windows application; learning objects may contain images, digital video, flash or other multimedia files.

A range of learning object standards exist, although these are becoming more closely aligned, with major VLE developers providing support for uploading learning objects according to defined standards. The creation of learning objects is also becoming easier, using sophisticated tools that integrate with Microsoft Office applications, such as PowerPoint.

Learning objects most often comprise short presentation-style resources, with some interactivity (e.g. user feedback). Although learning objects use HTML- and XML-based files for presentation purposes, it is also possible to use the learning object as a 'package' for displaying or delivering other files types, such as Word, PowerPoint etc.

Key principles of learning objects

The central aim of learning objects is to provide a standard for the creation of reusable content, allowing practitioners to develop course materials that are not dependent on any specific VLE system and that may be migrated or reused in other contexts.

There is little consensus on the definition or contextual purpose of learning objects, with a range of organisations advocating subtly different definitions; however, a few key principles may be summarised:

- Learning objects comprise a self-contained 'package' containing information, multimedia or other file types providing some form of integrated learning experience (e.g. a tutorial followed by self-assessment).

- Learning object 'packages' exist independently from larger systems and other content.

- Learning objects rely on web browsing technology, using HTML- and XML-based files for core information 'packaging'.

- Learning objects also rely on an intermediately application (e.g. a VLE or desktop application) to 'parse' and display the XML structure of the package.

- Learning objects are reusable (usable in a range of compatible systems).

- Learning objects may be created online or offline using appropriate software.

- Learning objects may be described using classification-style information (metadata) for user searching or other content management purposes.

Learning object standards and organisations

A number of organisations contribute to the development of learning object standards:

- *CETIS – Centre for Educational Technology Interoperability Standards (http://www.cetis.ac.uk)*. This JISC-funded group provides advocacy and discussion on interoperability standards in educational technology, including the IMS, SCORM and other e-learning standards.

- *IMS Global Learning Consortium (http://www.imsglobal.org)*. This organisation, developed by the US EDUCAUSE consortium, develops the IMS (instructional management system) standards for implementation of learning objects across a range of educational software; the IMS standard is based on several key specifications:

  - *'Specifications used to describe, discover and exchange content'*: these include 'metadata' for resource retrieval, 'content packaging' for resource management within differing e-learning systems and 'question and test' standards for assessments.

  - *'Specifications for content interaction and tracking'*: these include 'simple sequencing' to provide sequential frames or events within the learning object, 'competencies' for tracking learner achievement, 'learning design' to provide standards for learning object presentations and 'accessibility' to provide standards for accessible packages.

  - *'Specifications for application system interoperability'*: these include 'learner information package' to provide user profiles and 'enterprise' for sharing user profile information across differing systems (e.g. from FE to HE institutional VLEs).

- *SCORM (http://www.adlnet.org)*. SCORM, or shareable content object reference model is a standard for learning objects developed under the US Government Advanced Distributed Learning (ADL) initiative. The SCORM standard was originally designed as a medium for US defence training software, reflecting a self-paced, student-led approach for self-study. This pedagogical approach has drawn criticism from some organisations. The SCORM specification comprises several key features:

  - Shareable content objects (SCO): the basis of SCORM objects are individual learning packages containing 'assets' (e.g. images, multimedia, text, etc.).

  - the structure of the SCO package is organised using metadata to describe the location of 'assets' within the learning object.

- SCO objects may be imported/exported across compliant VLEs.
- Student tracking is possible to record attempt, scores, etc.
- Assessment recording may integrate with some VLEs.

Learning object software

- *Microsoft LRN Toolkit (http://www.microsoft.com/elearn/support .asp).* The free LRN tool (learning resource interchange) allows for the creation of learning object packages compliant with the IMS and SCORM standards. The LRN editor provides a hierarchical interface for adding resources and defining 'organisations' of content; the resulting files may be viewed in the LRN viewer or uploaded into other compliant systems.

- *Microsoft LRN Integration.* Once installed, the LRN application provides integration for Microsoft PowerPoint and FrontPage, allowing documents created in these applications to be 'saved as LRN' in either SCORM or IMS format.

- *Reload IMS SCORM Editor (http://www.reload.ac.uk).* This free editor may be used to create IMS- or SCORM-compliant packages; a viewer application is also provided.

- *Macromedia Authorware (http://www.macromedia.com).* This commercial product allows for the creation of SCORM-compliant learning objects via a graphical drag-and-drop interface; a simple 'wizard'-style interface may also be used to create resources, but training may be required for more advanced use.

VLE support for learning objects, content packaging, etc.

The specifications for IMS and SCORM are constantly under review, and support by various e-learning and VLE systems is similarly in constant development. The compatibility of learning object editors and publishing systems (e.g. VLEs) should be investigated thoroughly before serious use, including practical testing using a 'test' server.

Current VLE and other software support for IMS and other learning object standards may be found on the CETIS website (*http://www.cetis .ac.uk/directory/index_html?start=0*).

National Learning Network (NLN)

Currently, the UK Government is supporting the development of the National Learning Network materials (*http://www.nln.ac.uk*), a large repository of resources compliant with the learning object standards, many of which consist of short sequential activities, often including interactive features or self-assessment.

These resources may be viewed directly from the NLN website or may be downloaded for use in other systems, such as VLEs. A recent NLN report has been published outlining the UK Government's strategy for developing learning object standards for UK educational providers, in association with VLE developers; the report, *Paving the Way*, is available (*http://www.nln.ac.uk/materials/downloads/pdf/paving_the _way.pdf*).

NLN materials may also be accessed via the Middlesbrough College Materials Gateway, a fee-based service providing a structured portal to NLN materials arranged by subject; a 'Google'-style search is also available for searching the repository. The materials can be accessed directly from the gateway or linked from within a VLE. Information on obtaining access to the gateway may be obtained from Anthony Doyle, Middlesbrough College (e-mail: *a.doyle@mbro.ac.uk*).

Please see Appendix 1 for additional learning object repositories available on the Web.

Problems with learning objects

The use of learning object authoring software may present an appealing alternative to more established document formats within VLEs (e.g. Word, PDF); however, there are practical difficulties surrounding learning objects, including lack of compatibility across all VLE systems, lack of portability (i.e. ability to download, edit and easily print resources) and pedagogical debate over the capability or usability of learning objects as a serious solution for course delivery.

Consider this comment by Norm Frieson (2004):

To the knowledge of this author ... there have been no in-depth studies of the pedagogical consequences of these systems and ways of thinking, and no examinations of their epistemological and ideological implications. On a more practical level, others have noted a general lack of adoption of these techniques by both practitioners and vendors ... (p. 1)

Plagiarism

Plagiarism describes the unsolicited use of existing textual material from an original work without proper accreditation using a standard referencing method (such as the Harvard system); this could include use of a paragraph from a published text within an essay.

While a discussion of plagiarism is largely beyond the remit of this text, it may be worth considering some of the implications of plagiarism in the context of coursework submission, possibly via an e-learning system.

Automated systems now exist for the detection of documents containing plagiarised text. UK higher institutions are able to subscribe to the JISC plagiarism detection service, which allows staff to upload documents for automatic checking against a file store comprising the textual content of almost the entire Web. Details of the JISC plagiarism detection service are available (*http://online.northumbria.ac.uk/faculties/art/information_studies/Imri/Jiscpas/site/jiscpas.asp*).

Video conferencing

For study directed via distance learning, possibly over large geographical areas, e-learning systems may provide useful communication and course delivery functions. However, for person-to-person communication, rather than virtual interaction, the only option may be video conferencing.

Video conferencing involves the use of a specially designed conferencing studio, using a combination of video and computer technology to provide person-to-person communication via a viewing screen, microphones and cameras capable of focusing or 'zooming' on to particular speakers.

The JANET video conferencing switching service

(*http://www.jvcs.video.ja.net*)

Video conferencing is increasingly being delivered using web and Internet communications; the JANET video conferencing switching service

(JVCSS) provides a fast ISDN-based service across educational institutions within the JANET educational network system. Additionally, there are regional subnetworks in the UK for Wales (Welsh Video Network) and Scotland (Scottish MAN Videoconferencing Network).

A web booking service also exists to allow FE and HE institutes to request use of video conferencing facilities across the UK (*http://www.jvcs.ja.net/booking*).

Quality assurance and monitoring

Defining quality assurance for e-learning

The provision of quality, reliable and usable e-learning systems should be seen in the context of wider service delivery in the HE institution.

There is no simple definition or matrix for quality assurance in systems provision, but we can identify a range of operational factors in the deployment of e-learning systems that relate to quality issues:

- system selection criteria and fitness for purpose;
- provision of staff able to meet service management, service delivery, user training and related demands;
- system management and administration to achieve quality service provision;
- planning and strategy for achieving system aims, ambitions, etc.

There is a constant need to apprise current practices, including short- and long-term operational activity; aims of quality assurance typically include:

- setting benchmarks for service provision, through either internal or external standards;
- applying methods to compare current service provision against benchmarks, including human and computer processes or systems;
- providing reports on current service provision in relation to standards;
- applying methods to improve service provision;
- appraising the quality assurance process itself, including comparison or collaboration with external organisations and peer groups.

There is no simple, inclusive method for appraising the e-learning system as an institutional service; however, we may consider quality assurance under several key categories, including both generic and system-based approaches:

- *Quality assurance principles.* The basic values that define service provision, including issues such as customer care, provision of quality services and accessibility of services for users.

- *Policies and procedures.* Detailed guidelines for procedures in service provision.

- *Staffing.* Including the role and responsibilities of core e-learning staff.

- *System integrity and reliability.* Technical and operational reliability of systems and processes to ensure integral or fully functional software and content.

- *Standards compliance.* Issues for compliance with international, government and other standards for the provision of online systems.

- *System reports and statistics.* Use of reporting features for monitoring system usage and performance.

- *Feedback (workshops, surveys, interviews, etc.).* Use of person-to-person contact and other techniques to monitor user response to system use.

- *External accreditation.* Use of recognised schemes to obtain recognition of good practice.

- *External auditing.* Use of consultancy to provide feedback on service delivery.

Quality assurance principles

The basic principles driving the provision of quality services may be defined in the form of a mission or value statement. Although mission or value statements are usually seen in the context of an entire institution or information services department, there is no reason why this format may not be used to define e-learning service provision at the team or subdepartment level:

- The mission statement is usually a short statement or sentence outlining general aims for service delivery on a day-to-day basis, often in the context of user or customer needs and expectations.

- The value statement defines the ethical perspective of the service, dealing with issues such as provision of services on an equal basis for users or commitment to providing quality services.

It may also be useful to define more detailed quality assurance principles. Brockman (2003) defines a generic standard for benchmarking in the information sector:

- knowing the customer's needs – stated and/or implied;
- designing a service to meet them on or off the premises;
- faultless delivery of service;
- suitable facilities;
- good accommodation, seating, lighting, heating, etc;
- good 'housekeeping';
- reliant equipment – computers, videos;
- efficient administration ... queries answered efficiently and effectively;
- helpful courteous staff;
- efficient backup service;
- monitoring and evaluation including consumer expectations, complaints, recommendations for improvement ... ;
- feedback loops to build in improvement procedures and or checking that improvements are put in place. (pp. 5–6)

Other standards agencies in the HE sector also provide useful guidance for defining quality assurance principles. The Quality Assurance Agency (QAA) for Higher Education (2004) has published a report entitled *Code of practice for the assurance of academic quality and standards in higher education.*

Key aspects in the QAA guide for HE quality assurance include:

- a clear definition of responsibilities;
- consistent application of policies and practices that are underpinned by principles of fairness and equality of opportunity;
- the availability of clear and accessible information;
- the competence of staff;
- monitoring and review of policy, procedures and practices.

The full guide may be obtained at: *http://www.qaa.ac.uk/public/COP/ codesofpractice.htm.*

Although a definition of general service aims for the provision of quality systems is important, attention should also be given to specific methods and processes for benchmarking, testing and improving service provision.

Policies and procedures

The development of appropriate policy and procedure documents is an essential aspect of system deployment. Policy and procedure documents will provide standard procedures for carrying out routine operations within systems, defining the role and responsibility of core e-learning staff and other stakeholders.

Policies and procedures should reflect regular operational activity, but should also complement wider strategies such as an institutional learning and teaching strategy or other institutional policies, such as a complaints policy.

Policies and procedures might include:

- *policies on security, system abuse or misuse* – e.g. methods of 'locking' problematic features such as the ability to send mass e-mail or ability to modify personal details within systems;

- *policies on user account management* – e.g. methods for manual or automatic creation of accounts, management of incidental accounts and any procedures for accounts management based on system integration;

- *policies on training* – e.g. forms of training, including group formats for staff and students, or procedures for using teaching aids;

- *user responsibilities* – e.g. role of core e-learning staff, role of academic practitioners and other staff, including details of responsibilities such as accounts management, system maintenance or training provision;

- *procedures for user queries or complaints* – these may include procedures for dealing with enquiries, use of automated systems and enquiry tracking procedures.

Staffing

This aspect of quality assurance relates to the evaluation of staff practices and training needs, including methods for staff review and provision of continuing professional development (CPD).

A range of competencies, skills and disciplines may be seen in core e-learning staff and related support staff:

- customer care (i.e. dealing with users and the public);
- awareness of sector issues (e.g. HE issues, official bodies, sector trends);
- awareness of market base (i.e. knowledge of available software and computer hardware);
- awareness of standards, legislation and other sector recommendations;
- web development, programming and other technical skills;
- organisation of digital resources, including classification and indexing skills;
- academic liaison skills (i.e. mediating online service provision with the needs of academic practitioners);
- administrative skills (e.g. managing data within systems or in hardcopy formats);
- training, teaching and user support;
- project development skills;
- design and other graphical or presentational skills;
- research skills, including statistical reporting and analysis;
- management skills (i.e. managing others);
- collaborative and team working skills.

Quality assurance processes for e-learning staff will obviously occur within institutional or departmental guidelines; however, basic aspects of quality assurance for e-learning staff may include the following:

- appraisal of personal practice (including self-appraisal);
- identification of training needs;
- identification of appropriate CPD to fulfil training needs.

It is essential that the correct stakeholders provide input during appraisal of individual practice; appraisal processes should be grounded in institutional policy, relevance of staff functions and the wider staffing policies of the department. Key stakeholders may include:

- a human resources representative;
- senior departmental staff;
- the 'reviewee' (i.e. subject of appraisal).

Methods for appraisal may include:

- *self appraisal* – including use of personal logs, self-evaluation on key areas of practice or key skills, e.g. communication skills, organisational skills;
- *interviews* – these may allow the reviewee to discuss training needs with reviewers;
- *questionnaires/surveys* – these could provide a method to consider the status of reviewee development progress.

Although incidental training may be undertaken within the institute (e.g. BTEC diplomas, ECDL, PGCE), the provision of CPD should occur within the wider CPD framework of an appropriate professional body. In the case of library and information service staff, this will probably be represented by CILIP, the Chartered Institute of Library and Information Professionals (*http://www.cilip.org.uk*); other related professional bodies include the Higher Education Academy (*http://www.heacademy .ac.uk*) and the Institute of Learning and Teaching (now part of the HE Academy).

Provision of external accreditation/CPD is important for quality assurance and also for provision of appropriate staff development opportunities in an increasingly competitive employment market.

Further advice on quality assurance for staff development may be obtained from external standards bodies:

- *Higher Education Staff Development Agency* (*http://www.hesda.org .uk*). HESDA provides strategic advice, specialist resources and professional services for HE staff.
- *The Staff and Educational Development Association* (*http://www .seda.ac.uk*). SEDA is the professional association for staff and educational developers in the UK. SEDA's activities include conferences and events, publications, research and services to members.

- *CILIP* (*http://www.cilip.org.uk*). The Chartered Institute of Library and Information Professionals is the foremost UK-based professional body for library and information service (LIS) sector staff.
- *The Higher Education Academy* (*http://www.heacademy.ac.uk*). This professional body for HE practitioners and academic support staff was formed in 2004, combining the LTSN (Learning and Teaching Support Network), the ILT (Institute of Learning and Teaching) and other professional bodies.

For additional details on training, please see back to Chapter 4.

System integrity and reliability

Another aspect of quality assurance involves the physical integrity and reliability of systems. The institutional VLE or other web-based services will typically reside on in-house computer systems called servers – we can think of the VLE or web services in terms of a VLE server, a web server.

Procedures and systems should be in place to ensure system reliability, including aspects such as:

- maintaining online services 24 hours a day, 7 days a week;
- ensuring backup procedures are in place in the event of software or hardware failure;
- ensuring web-based content functions correctly, e.g. ensuring hyperlinks (URLs) are correct and not 'broken' and ensuring complex web-based systems function without errors or failure.
- ensuring backup procedures are documented and tested using a test server;
- ensuring adequate capacity is available within systems, e.g. sufficient hard-drive storage capacity, memory (RAM) or other appropriate hardware, typically meeting specifications recommended by a VLE company.

Methods to ensure system reliability will typically involve use of appropriate backup systems and software, including the following:

- *Tape drives*. Use of high-capacity data drive and tape media (resembling an audio cassette) may be used regularly to 'save' a snapshot of system data for later restoration in case of hardware or software failure.

- *Removable hard disks.* In the case of hardware failure, the actual hard disk containing all system data could be removed and installed in an identical machine; some hard drives are designed to allow easy removal, which is known as 'hot swapping'.

- *Hard disk redundancy.* Use of several hard drives may be possible to ensure data are retained in the event of a hard disk failure. The RAID system (redundant arrays of independent disks) is becoming a popular method to ensure data are available across several disk drives.

- *Use of local area network (LAN).* An image of the server computer could be stored for later recovery on another computer, and this data could simply be passed over the LAN.

It is also important to ensure the actual content of web-based systems (including VLEs) is maintained. 'Broken' links and dysfunctional features can result in a poor learning experience and prevent access to data.

Methods for ensuring the integrity of content include:

- *Links maintenance.* Academic staff will probably include hyperlinks within VLE systems or these may be present in conventional web pages, such as a student-focused website. Broken links may occur where a remote web address (URL) has changed or been removed; links could be checked manually by clicking on each link, but this can be laborious. Automatic link checking is possible within some VLEs using plug-ins and is possible on traditional websites using a link checker such as Xenu (*http://home.snafu.de/tilman/xenulink.html*).

- *Outdated information.* Calendars, announcements, time-tables and similar information should be reviewed periodically to remove outdated information and replaced as necessary. In some VLEs, it may be possible to achieve this kind of checking automatically – the Blackboard 'Announcement' system automatically shuffles notices in the announcement feature from the present day to 'last seven days', then 'last month', etc.

- *Metadata.* 'The current technical and fashionable term for bibliographic/descriptive data on the World Wide Web ...' (Catherall, 2000). Web-based resources should be described appropriately to ensure effective resource searching and retrieval. Traditional web pages (HTML files) may be simply described using the TITLE tag of the document, which is the most common form of descriptive data used by search engines; however, more complex descriptive and classification data may be added using META tags, e.g.:

<meta name="description" content="A Web site about ..." />

There are several basic META tags supported in HTML/XHTML that are used by some online search engines. For additional information on META tags, see the W3C schools tutorial (*http://www.w3schools .com/html/html_meta.asp*). More advanced META tags are recommended in the 'Dublin Core Metadata Element Set' and are also supported by some search engines (*http://dublincore.org*). Including metadata in HTML pages may improve the chances of users retrieving institute information using a web search engine such as Google, or improve search and retrieval processes using a search engine within an institutional website. Although these approaches are suitable for manually edited HTML files, this may not be possible within more complex systems; however, some VLEs such as Blackboard allow for inclusion of metadata to provide additional information for internal searching capabilities (provided via 'building blocks' extensions).

Standards compliance

System reliability and integrity are crucial factors in maintaining a quality service, but care should also be taken to ensure systems are compliant with relevant standards and legislation.

In Chapter 5, we noted issues for standards compliance in respect of accessibility legislation, including SENDA and industry standards provided by the W3C, including HTML/XHTML, CSS and the WCAG. Additionally we have considered the importance of copyright, data protection and other government legislation influencing the provision of HE services.

Methods to provide quality assurance for standards compliance could include the following:

- use of automated systems for checking W3C standards compliance in web-based resources, e.g. W3C Validators for XHTML and CSS (*http://www.w3c.com*), or the Bobby Validator for WCAG accessibility standards (*http://bobby.watchfire.com*);

- use of locally installed software for accessibility checking, including A-Prompt (*http://aprompt.snow.utoronto.ca*) or Useblenet's LIFT plug-in for Dreamweaver or FrontPage (*http://www.useablenet.com*);

- use of external auditing or consultancy;

- use of guidelines provided by official bodies within the HE sector, including the JISC Standards Information resource (*http://www.jisc .ac.uk/index.cfm?name=pub_ag_web*) or the TechDis guidelines for accessibility standards (*http://www.techdis.ac.uk/seven/precepts.html*).

For web standards auditing services (e.g. consultancy), see the final section of this chapter; for detailed web standards auditing specifications, see also Appendix 3.

System reports and statistics

Ensuring system performance may also involve examination of system reports available within the core operating system, VLE or other third-party reporting software.

Core Windows system information may provide useful information on server usage and performance; in some cases, excessive levels of memory, hard drive or processor usage may indicate inadequate system capacity for server processes and features.

Core Windows monitoring tools (available in most Windows servers such as Windows 2000 server, NT server, etc.) include the following:

- *Performance (Control Panel/Administrative Tools).* This tool provides access to 'System Monitor', displaying the current 'load' or usage of the system processor, hard disk and memory; the higher the load the more the server computer is being used. This tool allows for viewing reports in graph, text and other formats.

- *Event Viewer (Control Panel/Administrative Tools).* This tool provides system alerts indicating when applications or processes started, stopped or encountered errors; this tool is useful for locating the source of system problems.

- *Services (Control Panel/Administrative Tools).* This provides access to current 'Services' installed on the server; Services are like applications that have been installed, except they function as part of Windows (i.e. there is no need to 'run' service applications). Viewing Services is useful for discovering if Services have failed to start or have stopped.

- *Performance Logs and Alerts (Control Panel/Administrative Tools).* This alert tool provides performance information on aspects of the server, including the hard drive, disk cache (temporary hard drive space used for memory), system memory, processor performance and other aspects.

- *System Information (Start Button/Accessories).* This provides an overview of settings on the entire system, including possible DMA/IRQ conflicts (conflicting uses of system resources).

Some VLE systems also provide useful statistics to indicate usage of online courses or system features, such as user activity across VLE features over time. These reporting features may be used to analyse levels of activity on the VLE and often provide charts and other graphical representation of system usage.

Another key feature of some VLEs such as Blackboard is user 'tracking', which allows the online course manager to view usage of particular uploaded resources, including general trends and views for specific users/specific documents.

Alternative methods for monitoring traditional websites may include use of hit counters, recording trends in user access of particular web pages. Web tracking software should typically be installed on a networked server; web tracking software includes Webtrends (*http://www.webtrends.com*) and Deepmetrix (*http://www.deepmetrix.com*).

Feedback (workshops, surveys, interviews, etc.)

Quality assurance on wider service delivery may also be achieved via discussion and liaison with e-learning stakeholders. Consultation workshops may provide a useful forum to discuss a range of system delivery issues, such as student response to system usage, problems encountered by academic staff using system features or suggestions for system improvements. Interviews with senior staff may also provide a broader view of departmental response to system usage within learning and teaching processes.

Alternative methods of obtaining staff or student feedback could include surveys for user satisfaction, possibly delivered online via the VLE itself.

External accreditation

A wide range of external organisations provide external quality assurance in the form of accreditation and allocation of recognised awards.

Key accreditors include the following:

- *Quality Mark* (*http://www.legalservices.gov.uk/qmark*). This auditing service is provided by the government Community Legal Service (CLS), focusing on information services; this organisation awards a logo and statement of quality.

- *Charter Mark* (*http://www.chartermark.gov.uk*). This is a government-funded scheme for recognising excellence in public services. Six criteria are used for assessing the award (Charter Mark, 2004):

  1. setting standards and performing well;

  2. actively engage with your customers, partners and staff;

  3. be fair and accessible to everyone and promote choice;

  4. continuously develop and improve;

  5. use resources effectively and imaginatively;

  6. contribute to improving opportunities and quality of life in the communities you serve.

- *Investors in People* (*http://www.investorsinpeople.co.uk*). This is a national quality assurance body recognising quality 'human resource' practices and effective use of staff.

External auditing

Although government or other official quality assurance is possible, a wide range of commercial and third-party services exist for auditing service provision:

- *Direct Learn* (*http://www.directlearn.co.uk*). Direct Learn (UK) provides consultancy for e-learning project management, strategic policy development, online service evaluation and website usability and accessibility reviews.

- *National Register of Access Consultants (http://www.nrac.org.uk/).* This database service provides details on accessibility consultants for a wide range of accessibility issues, including electronic systems.

It can therefore be seen that quality assurance for e-learning systems is not a single process or activity, but comprises a range of considerations, including staffing, system integrity and external auditing.

Conclusion

The HE environment is changing rapidly, with increasing pressure on information services to meet the demands of an increasingly non-traditional context. Many of these changes are widely acknowledged, including the rise of the Internet, growing user or client diversity and the wide ranging impact of recent legislation. However, it may be worth considering a few evident trends in HE and IT that may shape e-learning in the near future.

Worldwide e-learning

Increasing network connectivity from the home, workplace and public services has led to the development of the Internet as a cost-effective and international communications channel.

The potential of this global market is clearly being realised by commercial organisations, including providers of educational services. Companies such as Thomson NetG (*http://www.netg.com*) are providing online training accredited by industry leaders (such as Microsoft) to meet the needs of a worldwide user base in computing and technical skills. Traditional educational institutions have also realised the potential of the global 'net' market, such as the Norwegian university NKI (*http://www.nki.no/in_english.xsql*) and WUN, the Worldwide Universities Network (*http://www.wun.co.uk*) delivering HE courses online.

Similarly, the UK government has funded the development of the 'UK eUniversity Project', delivering HE from UK universities for a global market via distance learning (unfortunately now disbanded).

The characteristics of this new global educational market are characterised by distance learning, student-led study approaches and use of VLE systems to provide communication, collaboration and content delivery functions.

The provision of higher education for the international community is already a thriving industry in the UK. The predominance of the English language and prestige of UK and US universities has given these countries an early advantage in harnessing the potential of the global education market; a recent report by the British Council (2004) demonstrates the scale of overseas university applicants, with overseas demand for places expected to rise in the future:

> There are currently over 35,000 international students undertaking research in UK universities, making a major contribution to the high quality of the UK's research output. This number could more than double by 2020 ... (*http://www.britishcouncil.org*)

The report, *Vision 2020: Forecasting International Student Mobility*, suggests that action is necessary to expand capacity and systems for overseas university applicants, or UK universities will lose possible revenue of up to £1.3 billion per annum:

> Over 500,000 international students are estimated to come to the UK each year to study English. The total value of this sector is £1.3 billion pa to the UK ...

Investment in infrastructure for traditional on-campus course delivery will be an important requirement to meet the demands of increasing overseas demand; however, it will also be necessary to develop the infrastructure to support an inevitable expansion of distance-learning-based courses, involving use of VLE and other e-learning tools. The report comments:

> The UK is currently the global leader in delivering accredited Higher Education to international students in their own countries through distance learning and related arrangements. The numbers are predicted to grow from the current about 200,000 students to some 800,000 by 2020.

Whether UK HE is able to take advantage of this growing demand from the international community remains to be seen, especially considering the collapse of the UK E-University in 2003; however, several major UK universities continue to participate in WUN, the Worldwide Universities Network.

E-learning systems will obviously play an important role in delivering education in a remote context, raising the importance of VLE development issues, such as interface customisation for multilingual display and development of support systems to meet overseas student needs.

Meeting skills demands

It is widely accepted that employment today is far different than the 'trades and industry'-based work of previous generations. The current employment market is characterised by smaller commercial organisations, predominance of light manufacturing and information-focused services.

Although the diversity of employment opportunities has never been greater, many appointments provide only short-term security, with increasing use of fixed-term contracts. The importance of employee training to meet the demands of a flexible and uncertain job market is proving vital both for retraining in the event of career change and for providing relevant skills in a climate of rapid technological development.

The impetus for industry-focused training is clearly demonstrated in recent government reports and recommendations, such as the government White Paper *The Future of Higher Education* (2003), and *Foundation Degrees – Meeting the Need for Higher Skill Levels* (2003):

> This is the era of lifelong learning with adults returning to learning – full time or part time – often on more than one occasion in their lifetime in order to refresh their knowledge, upgrade their skills and sustain their employability ... (*Foundation Degrees – Meeting the Need for Higher Skill Levels*, 2003)

E-learning will play an important role in facilitating low-contact, part-time study necessitated by increasing employee participation in HE; although this model for using e-learning is already a feature of HE, it remains to be seen if this will become the dominant form of HE study, with full-time study becoming increasingly expensive and the possibility of 'top-up fees' in addition to conventional fees for university entrants.

The e-tutor

The growth in low-contact teaching, for increasing part-time study, distance learning and blended approaches, will inevitably lead to increasing dependence on electronic communication systems; this will inevitably translate into increasing demands on teaching staff to respond to student queries via asynchronous features such as e-mail, discussion forums and synchronous features such as real-time chat.

Student support models may shift significantly from traditional class or tutorial contact to electronic support systems, characterised by largely unlimited and unrestricted access in the form of e-learning systems. Obviously, strategies for managing and regulating student and tutor interaction will be vital for ensuring effective online course delivery.

A range of methods for managing user support are currently available in current VLEs; discussion forums could be used for student queries, allowing tutors to respond to messages at a convenient time, preserving both question and response for viewing by other students. Use of an auto-response e-mail could also be used to respond instantly to student e-mail queries; this e-mail could contain basic system help or links to academic support material, allowing the tutor to prioritise e-mail queries and respond personally if queries are beyond the scope of the auto-response.

The current role of the tutor as 'online course manager' usually includes a wide range of activities, including use of the e-learning management interface to upload course materials, manage user access to online courses and interact with students via communication features. With rising demand for low-contact study and a predicated growth in distance learning, the role of individual tutors may require more precise definition or specialisation to meet the administrative demands of a larger student base.

Academic support staff are often used in a limited capacity to manage online courses, including user management, organisation of course content and some student enquiry support; this role could be expanded in the future to allow academic staff added time for pedagogical activities, such as course material creation or interaction with students.

As VLE systems integrate more closely with core institutional systems, some operational functions may also be carried out by other administrative staff within the institute (e.g. user registry, admissions).

Additionally, specialism within academic functions may define particular roles such as online course design, content creation or user support.

Mobile learning (m-learning)

The success of the portable cell phone and SMS (short messaging service) has demonstrated the functionality of portable communication devices. It is now possible to access Internet resources using similar portable devices using a LAN or long-range 'wireless' network services.

Portable (wireless) network access is possible using a range of equipment:

- *Laptop (notebook computer).* The conventional laptop allows for portability because it is usually less heavy than a desktop computer, providing an integrated keyboard, retractable monitor and latest hardware and graphics capabilities. Additionally, the laptop provides access to removable media drives such as CD-R (writable CD), CD-RW (re-writable CD) or even DVD. Most laptops provide access to typical Windows software, including web browser and Internet features. Since the laptop comprises a fully featured computer, this inevitably means the laptop is still too large to use in a hand-held capacity. However, the laptop is still an appealing compromise between traditional computing functionality and portability; additionally, mini laptops are also available, providing high performance and typical computing features while being almost as portable as a 'personal organiser'. Typical laptop computers require a wireless network adapter to connect to wireless networks.

- *PDA (personal digital assistant).* These devices provide a complete operating system, such as Microsoft Windows, within a small, hand-held system. PDAs provide a compact digital display and provide a range of 'input' features, including: miniature integrated keyboard, a larger external keyboard, shortcut buttons to activate a menu interface, voice recognition and handwriting recognition (using an on-screen stylus). PDAs also allow for use of a standard web browser, such as Microsoft Internet Explorer. Although PDAs provide a range of typical Windows functionality, including software applications, the user interface is somewhat small and does not provide a completely satisfactory alternative to a conventional PC for data entry and other usual tasks. However, the PDA is most useful for incidental computing activities and communication features, providing e-mail, web access and other interactive features, all within an interface roughly the size of a mobile phone.

- *WAP (wireless access protocol) phone.* The mobile phone already provides SMS and voice-based communication; however, WAP-enabled phones also allow for limited web browsing capability using a 'mini browser', providing a text-based, menu-driven interface. WAP-phones also provide e-mail and SMS messaging. Whereas laptops and more recent hand-held PDA computers may access typical HTML resources using standard web browsers (e.g. Internet Explorer), WAP devices rely on a new wireless mark up language (WML) and may only access and display wireless/WAP networked sites. However, support for WAP among major websites is growing. To see what a WAP site looks like, try the BBC WAP emulator: *http://www.bbc.co.uk/mobile/web/emulator.html*

- *WAP pager.* These devices are used to send and receive short SMS messages; a WAP-compliant pager may also be used to connect to a WAP website via a 'mini browser'.

Currently, there are several basic methods to access networked resources via portable devices:

- *Short range.* Conventional LANs provide access to network resources and external Internet access via networked PCs; in the university of the future, static networked terminals located in fixed areas like IT labs will be replaced with portable laptops and other mobile devices, connected to the LAN via wireless networking rather than conventional cables. Imagine a student able to use their hand-held PDA computer to send e-mails or check class timetables while having lunch in the refectory, or collaborating with other students in a common area using wireless-enabled laptops to research a project.

    The wireless LAN (WiLAN) uses a 'wireless gateway' to transmit conventional LAN services to the user's portable device. Obviously, short-range wireless networking only functions within the limited range of the local network radio signal. WiLAN may also provide full Internet access to the World Wide Web via a conventional web browser.

- *Long range.* This essentially provides Internet access for mobile devices, and is not dependent on an in-house transmitter (i.e. not restricted to access within a small area, but across a much wider area, such as a city, depending on the limitation of ISP services available). Unlike WiLAN (local wireless networks), long-range wireless Internet using a PDA or WAP device is generally very slow, although configuring the browser for text-only mode will optimise downloading.

Most Internet-enabled mobile phones use WAP to access WAP-compliant sites. WAP phones can only access WAP sites and cannot simply browse the World Wide Web. However, the hand-held PDA may be used to access the Internet and websites via a mobile phone (using an internal modem) and a mobile network standard such as GPRS (General Packet Radio Service).

The use of mobile technology may have significant educational uses, such as integration with e-learning systems for student announcements and wider access to e-mail for communication with staff or students.

Obvious limitations exist in the use of some portable devices, such as WAP and PDA, including limited WAP Internet access and reduced interface size; however, future mobile devices will probably complement desktop computing rather than replace desktop PCs, providing integrated voice, e-mail, SMS messaging, web browsing and other graphical features such as digital video. The latest PDA devices ('smart phones') are already incorporating many of these features.

Ubiquitous e-learning

With increasing dependence on e-learning systems and growing availability of mobile networked computing, students will increasingly access online study in a diverse range of contexts.

Currently, the majority of e-learning activities within educational institutions are restricted to use of static networked terminals (i.e. connected via cabling to a network socket). The advent of WiLANs is allowing the use of portable computer devices such as laptops or PDAs at any location within the HE institution, for example allowing students to log in to institutional systems, such as a VLE in the lecture theatre, refectory or any other location within the wireless transmission range.

The rise of portable and hand-held networked devices may also widen access to institutional systems outside the academic institution; for example, a 'smart phone' could access institutional email, calendaring systems or even a WAP-enabled VLE.

Although current laptop computers are widely used for limited portable computing, the handheld device has the advantage of easy portability, with latest models combining phone and SMS functionality with PDA-style Internet access and personal computing functionality.

It is not hard to imagine how a PDA-style device could be used to support conventional computing for checking course announcements, emailing tutors or even editing textual course work.

E-learning devices of the future

Internet connectivity is now possible using a range of mobile devices, such as mobile phones and pagers; additionally, other established technology is also incorporating Internet functionality. However, it remains to be seen to what extent integration of networked access will remain proprietary and how far systems will go towards mutual compatibility.

Some of the following devices are widely available; others are not yet widely available, but in developmental stages:

- *TV-based Internet.* Although not widely available at present, web browsing via a TV screen could become the most popular method of using the World Wide Web in the future, integrating conventional satellite and cable TV with features such as e-mail and web browsing.

- *Games stations.* Some games consoles, such as the PlayStation 2, provide capability for fast broadband Internet access; although this is intended primarily for gaming, console networking could also be used to access conventional web services.

- *Smart phone.* The hand-held PDA computer and conventional mobile phone are becoming increasingly integrated, with portable devices providing combined e-mail, voice, SMS, Internet and other functionality.

- *Multimedia systems.* Integration of audio, video, DVD, radio and other 'multimedia' systems is now available; it is not to hard to imagine the inclusion of e-mail, web functionality and other communication features within these entertainment systems, providing an entirely integrated communications system to replace the distinct TV, computer and other appliances available today. The Microsoft WebTV is a current example of this kind of product, providing TV, multimedia and Internet functionality via the same 'TV' appliance.

Some thoughts

E-learning is not strictly an emerging technology, nor it is a well-defined pedagogical field or discipline; instead, e-learning describes our current attempts to reconcile a rapidly changing educational climate with technological innovation.

In this respect, it is important to consider the broad spectrum of available technology for learning and teaching, evaluating software on the basis of usability, functionality and relevance to educational context.

The future of e-learning is not entirely predictable; much will depend on the future track record and performance of VLE systems across UK institutions. The resilience, pedagogical effectiveness and access-ibility of educational technology will demand important research in coming years.

Additionally, it is not clear whether Internet access will remain in the conventional computer-based context of the present, or whether emerging alternatives, such as TV and games consoles, will provide closer integration between traditional entertainment systems, multimedia computing and Internet connectivity.

E-learning systems also offer the possibility for sharing educational content across the academic community, including lecture presentations, subject-specific guides or interactive assessments. The emergence of IMS and other models for reusable learning objects will allow educators to upload 'packaged' teaching resources into a wide range of compatible VLE systems. It remains to be seen to what extent this technology will allow for collaboration and resource sharing across the educational community, in the context of intellectual property and copyright legislation.

Perhaps the last word on e-learning's future should rest with the inventor of the Web, Tim Berners-Lee (2004), in a statement which raises the question on the reusability of e-learning materials and global access for the international community:

> I hope that educators will pool their resources and create a huge supply of online materials. I hope much of this will be available freely to those especially in developing countries who may not have access to it any other way. Then I think we will see two things. One will be that keeping that web of material up to date will take a lot of time and effort – it will seem like more effort than creating it in the first place. The other is that we will see how essential people, and their wisdom, and their personal interactions, are to the educational process.

It is hoped this text has provided some insight into the emerging world of e-learning, virtual learning environments and related technology.

Comments on this text are always welcome by the author at: *elearning@draigweb.co.uk*. Readers are also referred to the 'E-learning Information Portal', which is maintained as a complementary resource for this text (*http://elearning.draigweb.co.uk*).

Appendix 1
E-learning online (selected URLs)

This information is also available online and updated at: *http://elearning .draigweb.co.uk.* (The online version is an open resource, which may be updated – e-mail *elearning@draigweb.co.uk* for login information.)

Accessibility applications and systems

- Accessible Web Publishing Wizard For Microsoft Office (converts PowerPoint, Word, etc., to accessible HTML): *http://cita.rehab.uiuc .edu/software/office/omp_welcome.html*
- A-Prompt (website validator): *http://aprompt.snow.utoronto.ca*
- A Real Validator (Web Design Group application for HTML/XHTML validation): *http://arealvalidator.com/*
- Betsie (text-only/accessible display script): *http://betsie.sourceforge .net*
- Bobby – a Watchfire product (website validator): *http://bobby .watchfire.com*
- LIFT for Dreamweaver/Frontpage (website accessibility support tool): *http://www.useablenet.com*
- Patsie (commercial text-only display adaptation of Betsie): *http:// www.tagish.co.uk/products/patsie*
- Text-transcoder (website text-only display system): *http://www .useablenet.com*

Accessibility bodies

- British Dyslexia Association: *http://www.bda-dyslexia.org.uk*
- Disability Rights Commission: *http://www.drc-gb.org*

- Equal Opportunities Commission: *http://www.eoc.org.uk*
- EuroAccessibility (developing a European accessibility standard): *http://www.euroaccessibility.org/*
- RNIB (Royal National Institute for the Blind): *http://www.rnib.org*

Accessibility support sites

- Microsoft Accessibility: *http://www.microsoft.com/enable*
- Techdis (disability support FE/HE): *http://techdis.ac.uk*
- TechDis resources for accessibility standards: *http://www.techdis .ac.uk/seven/precepts.html*
- Web Accessibility Initiative (WAI): *http://www.w3.org/WAI*
- W3C Web Content Accessibility Guidelines (WCAG): *http://www .w3.org/TR/WAI-WEBCONTENT*

Accessibility and standards validation online (also see web standards ...)

- Bobby – a Watchfire product (website validator): *http://bobby .watchfire.com*
- W3C CSS Validator: *http://jigsaw.w3.org/css-validator*
- W3C HTML/XHTML Validator: *http://www.htmlhelp.com/tools/ validator*
- W3C Mark-Up Validation Service: *http://validator.w3.org*

Accessibility auditing services

- Direct Learn: *http://www.directlearn.co.uk*
- National Register of Access Consultants: *http://www.nrac.org.uk*

Assessment software (also see VLEs)

- Questionmark Perception (assessment system): *http://www .questionmark.com*
- Testwise (Learnwise assessments): *http://www.learnwise.com*

Assistive technology

- Dolphin Products (Supernova screen magnifier and Braille display, HAL screen reader and Braille display, Lunar/LunarPlus screen magnifiers): *http://www.dolphinuk.co.uk/products/*
- JAWS screen reader: *http://www.freedomscientific.com/fs_products/ software_jaws.asp*
- Microsoft Accessibility Tools: *http://www.microsoft.com/enable*

Copyright

- CLA (Copyright Licensing Agency): *http://www.cla.co.uk*
- Educational Recording Agency (ERA): *http://www.era.org.uk*
- FERL Copyright Resources: *http://ferl.becta.org.uk/display.cfm?resID =4972*
- Newspaper Licensing Agency (NLA): *http://www.nla.co.uk*
- UK Patents Office: *http://www.patent.gov.uk*

Document authoring applications and viewers

- Adobe Acrobat PDF: *http://www.acrobat.com*
- Microsoft Office: *http://office.microsoft.com*
- Open Office: *http://www.openoffice.org*
- Star Office: *http://wwws.sun.com/software/star/staroffice*

Education bodies

- ALT (Association for Learning Technology): *http://www.alt.ac.uk*
- ELWa (Education and Learning Wales): *http://www.elwa.ac.uk*
- Higher Education Academy: *http://www.heacademy.ac.uk*
- LSC (Learning and Skills Council): *http://www.lsc.gov.uk*
- LSDA (Learning and Skills Development Agency): *http://www.lsda .org.uk/*
- LTSN (Learning and Teaching Support Network): *http://www.ltsn .ac.uk*
- NIACE (National Institute of Adult Continuing Education): *http:// www.niace.org.uk*

E-learning/educational technology support bodies (also see Pedagogy)

- ALT (Association for Learning Technology): *http://www.alt.ac.uk*
- BECTa (British Educational Communications & Technology Agency): *http://www.becta.org.uk*
- Bristol Learning Technology Support Service (e-learning pages): *http://www.ltss.bris.ac.uk/elearning*
- Bristol Learning Technology Support Service (LTSS): *http://www .ltss.bris.ac.uk*
- CSILE – Computer Supported Intentional Learning Environments: *http://csile.oise.utoronto.ca*
- Edutools: *http://www.edutools.com*
- European Institute of E-Learning (EIfEL): *http://www.eife-l.org/*
- FERL (Further Education Resources for Learning): *http://ferl.becta .org.uk/*
- JISC (The Joint Information Systems Committee): *http://www .jisc.ac.uk*
- LTSN Centre for Information and Computer Science: *http://www.ics .ltsn.ac.uk/*
- NILTA (National Information and Learning Technologies Association): *http://www.nilta.org.uk*

- NLN (National Learning Network): *http://www.nln.ac.uk*
- UCISA (Universities and Colleges Information Systems Association): *http://www.ucisa.ac.uk*

Enquiry systems

- Trackit: *http://www.itsolutions.intuit.com*
- Virtual Reference Toolkit: *http://www2.tutor.com/products/vrt.aspx*

Government, official bodies and national statistics agencies

- British Council: *http://www.britishcouncil.org*
- Department for Education and Skills: *http://www.dfes.gov.uk*
- Public Technology.net (e-government and public sector IT news): *http://www.publictechnology.net*
- HESA (Higher Education Statistics Agency): *http://www.hesa.ac.uk/*
- HMSO (Her Majesty's Stationery Office – government publications): *http://www.hmso.gov.uk*
- LISU (Library & Information Statistics Unit): *http://www.lboro.ac .uk/departments/dils/lisu/lisuhp.html*
- NLN (National Learning Network): *http://www.nln.ac.uk*
- ONS (Office of National Statistics): *http://www.statistics.gov.uk*

Information science/management resources (general portals)

- Info Connect (a general information science and management portal): *http://www.lwrw.com*

International e-learning bodies

- Commonwealth of Learning: *http://www.col.org*
- EDUCAUSE: *http://www.educause.edu/*

- EuroAccessibility (developing a European accessibility standard): *http://www.euroaccessibility.org*
- European Institute of E-Learning (EIfEL): *http://www.eife-l.org/*
- International Forum of Educational Technology & Society: *http://ifets.ieee.org/maillist.html*
- Prometeus (European Union e-learning agency): *http://www.prometeus.org*
- Worldwide Universities Network e-learning portal: *http://www.wun.ac.uk/elearning/index.html*

Journals (online) and e-zines

- Ariadne (Information Science e-journal): *http://www.ariadne.ac.uk*
- Edutools (Educational Technology Reviews): *http://www.edutools.com*
- E-Learning Knowledge Base: *http://ekb.mwr.biz*
- Information for Social Change: *http://www.libr.org/ISC/links.html*
- Information Research: *http://informationr.net/ir/*
- Internet Resources Newsletter: *http://www.hw.ac.uk/libwww/irn/irn115/irn115.html*
- Managing Information: *http://www.managinginformation.com/*
- Online Journal of Distance Learning Administration: *http://www.westga.edu/%7Edistance/jmain11.html*

Learning object applications

- Macromedia Authorware: *http://www.macromedia.com*
- Microsoft LRN Toolkit: *http://www.microsoft.com/elearn/support.asp*
- Reload IMS/SCORM Editor: *http://www.reload.ac.uk*

Learning object repositories

- Brite Ideas (Key Stage 1 & 2 resources): *http://www.icbl.hw.ac.uk/ltdi/*
- Curriculum Online (statutory education resources): *http://www.curriculumonline.gov.uk*
- HEAL (Health Education Assets Library): *http://www.healcentral.org/*
- iLumina (undergraduate science tutorials): *http://turing.bear.uncw.edu/iLumina/index.asp*
- MERLOT (Multimedia Educational Resource for Learning and Teaching): *http://www.merlot.org/Home.po*
- Netskills – TONIC (IT training resources): *http://www.netskills.ac.uk/TonicNG/cgi/sesame?lng*
- NLN (National Learning Network) Materials: *http://www.nln.ac.uk/materials/tutors/browse_materials.asp*
- NSDL (National Science Digital Library): *http://nsdl.org*
- RDN (Resource Discovery Network) Virtual Training Suite: *http://www.vts.rdn.ac.uk*
- Thompson Net G (mainly IT tutorials): *http://www.netg.com*
- W3C Schools (web development tutorials): *http://www.w3schools.com*

Multimedia applications

- Goldwave: *http://www.goldwave.com*
- RealAudio Player/Tools: *http://www.real.com*
- Windows Movie Maker: *http://www.microsoft.com/windowsxp/moviemaker/*

Pedagogy/e-learning academic practice

- Association for Learning Technology: *http://www.alt.ac.uk*
- Distance Learning Research (JISC e-mail list): *http://www.jiscmail.ac.uk/lists/DISTANCELEARN-RESEARCH.html*

- E-learning Post: *http://www.elearningpost.com*
- International Forum of Educational Technology & Society: *http://ifets.ieee.org/maillist.html*
- LTSN (Learning and Teaching Support Network): *http://www.ltsn.ac.uk*
- Masie Center: *http://www.masie.com/*
- Networked Learning (JISC email forum): *http://www.jiscmail.ac.uk/lists/NETWORKED-LEARNING.html*
- Node Learning Technologies Network: *http://thenode.org*
- Online Pedagogy Portal: *http://careers.lancs.ac.uk/pb/net-lit.htm*
- Teaching and Learning with Network Technologies: *http://www.le.ac.uk/TALENT*
- The Computer Assisted Assessment Centre: *http://www.caacentre.ac.uk/*
- Teaching On-line (JISC e-mail forum): *http://www.jiscmail.ac.uk/lists/TEACHING-ON-LINE.html*

Presentation tools

- Boxmind Flashpoint: *http://www.boxmind.com/products/flashpoint*
- Impatica for PowerPoint and Director: *http://www.impatica.com*
- Microsoft Producer for PowerPoint: *http://www.microsoft.com/windows/windowsmedia/technologies/producer.asp*

Plagiarism detection systems

- JISC Plagiarism Detection Service: *http://online.northumbria.ac.uk/faculties/art/information_studies/Imri/Jiscpas/site/jiscpas.asp*
- Turntin (system used by JISC): *http://www.turnitin.com/*

Professional bodies

- ASLIB (Association for Information Management): *http://www.aslib.co.uk/*
- CILIP (Chartered Institute of Library and Information Professionals): *http://www.cilip.org.uk*
- Higher Education Academy: *http://www.heacademy.ac.uk*

Suppliers and resellers

- Chest (supplier for educational systems): *http://www.chest.ac.uk*

Training providers/resources and staff development bodies

- ECDL (European Computer Driving Licence): *http://www.ecdl.co.uk*
- Netskills (IT/e-learning training materials): *http://www.netskills.ac.uk*
- Online Education and Training (a distance learning course for educators either available over ten weeks by distance learning or four weeks, intensive study, delivered by the Institute of Education at the University of London): *http://www.ioe.ac.uk/english/OET2.htm*
- Solent Training & Development/Virtual Learning Centre: *http://www.solentbiz.co.uk*
- SEDA (Staff and Educational Development Association): *http://seda.ac.uk*
- Thompson Net G (mainly IT tutorials): *http://www.netg.com*
- TONIC (Netskills): *http://www.netskills.ac.uk/TonicNG/cgi/sesame?tng*
- W3C Schools Web Tutorials: *http://www.w3schools.com*

VLE manuals and guides

Note: Please contact relevant organisations to obtain permission before reusing any material.

- Blackboard Guides (University of East Anglia): *http://www.uea.ac.uk/ltg/blackboard*
- Bodington Training Manuals (Leeds University): *http://www.fldu.leeds.ac.uk/site/gatehouse/information/docs/*
- Bodington guides (Oxford University Weblearn project; NB. Login as 'visitor'): *https://www.weblearn.ox.ac.uk/bodington/site/info/docs/guides*
- Learnwise user guide (Solent training): *http://www.solent.ac.uk/ExternalUP/225/userguide.pdf*
- Teknical Virtual Campus Guides (Western Colleges Consortium): *http://www.westerncc.ac.uk/howdoi.html*
- WebCT official guides, tutorials and downloadable manuals: *http://www.webct.com/communities*
- WebCT manuals (Leeds Metropolitan University): *http://www.lmu.ac.uk/teaching/webct/documents/manuals.htm*

Translation systems

- Babelfish: *http://www.babelfish.com*
- Translation Experts: *http://www.tranexp.com*

Video conferencing

- The Janet Video-conferencing Switching Service: *http://www.jvcs.video.ja.net*

VLEs/e-learning systems (commercial)

- Blackboard: *http://www.blackboard.com*
- ClassCampus: *http://www.classcampus.com*

- FD Learning: *http://www.fdlearning.com*
- FirstClass: *http://www.firstclass.com*
- Learnwise: *http://www.learnwise.net*
- Lotus Learning Space: *http://www.lotus.com/products/learnspace .nsf/wdocs/homepage*
- Merlin: *http://www.hull.ac.uk/elearning/merlin*
- Teknical Virtual Campus: *http://www.teknical.com*
- Virtual-U: *http://www.vlei.com*
- WebCT Campus: *http://www.webct.com*

VLEs/e-learning systems (not for profit)

- ATutor: *http://www.atutor.ca*
- Bodington: *http://www.bodington.org*
- Claroline: *http://www.claroline.net*
- Colloquia e-learning software: *http://www.colloquia.net*
- Co-mentor: *http://comentor.hud.ac.uk/*
- COSE: *http://www.staffs.ac.uk/COSE/*
- Fle 3: *http://fle3.uiah.fi/*
- Jones E-Education: *http://www.jonesadvisorygroup.com/*
- Moodle: *http://www.moodle.org*

Web authoring applications and resources

- Macromedia Contribute: *http://www.macromedia.com*
- Macromedia Dreamweaver MX: *http://www.macromedia.com*
- Macromedia Homesite: *http://www.macromedia.com*
- W3C Schools (web development tutorials): *http://www.w3schools .com*
- W3C Web Content Accessibility Guidelines (WCAG): *http://www.w3 .org/TR/WAI-WEBCONTENT*

Web browsers

- Amaya: *http://www.w3.org/amaya*
- Internet Explorer: *http://www.microsoft.com/ie*
- Lynx (a text-only browser): *http://www.lynx.browser.org*
- Mozilla: *http://www.mozilla.org*
- Netscape Navigator: *http://www.netscape.com*
- Opera: *http://www.opera.com*

Web standards organisations and guidelines

- CETIS (Centre for Educational Technology Interoperability Standards): *http://www.cetis.ac.uk*
- IEEE Computer Society Learning Technology Task Force (LTTF): *http://lttf.ieee.org/*
- IMS (Instructional Management System) Global Learning Consortium: *http://www.imsglobal.org*
- JISC – web standards and guidance: *http://www.jisc.ac.uk/index.cfm? name=pub_ag_web*
- Section 508 Rehabilitation Act Guidelines: *http://www.section508 .gov*
- Shareable Content Object Reference Model (SCORM): *http://www .adlnet.org*
- The World Wide Web Consortium (W3C): *http://www.w3c.org*
- W3C User Agent Accessibility Guidelines 1.0 (UAAG): *http://www .w3.org/TR/UAAG10/*
- W3C Web Content Accessibility Guidelines (WCAG): *http://www .w3.org/TR/WAI-WEBCONTENT/*

Appendix 2
VLE questionnaire for case histories

This questionaire was issued to HE instructions across the UK, winter 2003/2004:

1. Your name and job title (optional and confidential).
2. Your organisation name.
3. Approximately how many full/part-time students attend your institution?
4. What is the main VLE system at your institution and when did you purchase it?
5. Did you have a method for publishing educational materials online before obtaining your VLE? If so please describe.
6. Please describe briefly up to four criteria which influenced your choice of VLE system.
7. Did you install the VLE internally, or did you purchase third-party consultancy? Please describe.
8. Please describe briefly any significant technical problems or challenges in installing your VLE.
9. Does your VLE integrate with any other web interface (such as an MLE 'managed learning environment' or institutional website)? Please describe.
10. Does your VLE integrate with any other systems (e.g. user login database or course records)?
11. Do you have a learning and teaching strategy or online learning strategy? Please indicate any relationship between the two.
12. Do you have a dedicated team to manage or support your VLE? Please briefly describe their role and capacity.

13. To what extent do staff outside your department support VLE delivery (e.g. tutors, department administrators)?

14. To what extent is your VLE used to support distance learning, part-time courses or other non-conventional teaching methods?

15. To what extent is your VLE used by academic departments across the institution?

16. What were the barriers or challenges in promoting VLE use across academic departments.

17. What do you consider to be the most important features or functions provided by the VLE for teaching and learning across your institution?

18. Additional comments (optional). Please describe any other significant issue(s) in delivering your VLE.

Appendix 3
Checklist for accessibility/standards compliance

This appendix contains information on standards compliance for web resources. Attendance of a basic course in HTML would be a useful precursor to implementing the following procedures. Tutorials on many aspects of web development are also available at the World Wide Web Consortium's 'W3Schools' site (*http://www.w3schools.com/*). Please refer to the Glossary of terms for acronyms or other technical terms.

This appendix is split into the following sections:

1. *Online resources at a glance.* Key URLs of online tools and guidelines.

2. *General notes.* A few important issues to consider before undertaking standards/accessibility auditing.

3. *Mark-up/CSS standards compliance.* A few pointers for auditing HTML/ XHTML resources and CSS.

4. *Web Content Accessibility Guidelines 1.0 (WCAG).* When your mark-up and CSS is valid, you should perform accessibility auditing.

5. *Bobby Accessibility Validation.* A brief guide to the Windows application and online version of this automatic accessibility auditing tool.

6. *Other validation methods.* Describes alternative tools and methods to ensure web resources are usable in a range of contexts.

Section 1: Online resources at a glance

- Bobby Accessibility Validator (WCAG/US 508): *http://bobby .watchfire.com/*
- W3C CSS Specifications Level 1: *http://www.w3.org/TR/REC-CSS1/*

- W3C CSS Specifications Level 2: *http://www.w3.org/TR/REC-CSS2/*
- W3C CSS Validator: *http://jigsaw.w3.org/css-validator/*
- W3C mark-up specifications (HTML/ XHTML): *http://www.w3.org/ MarkUp/*
- W3C Mark-up Validation Service (online): *http://validator.w3.org/*
- W3Schools (tutorials for web development): *http://www.w3schools .com/*
- Web Design Group Mark-up Validator – online version (supports multiple 'batch' checking): *http://www.htmlhelp.com/tools/validator/*
- Web Design Group Mark-up Validator – Windows application ('a real validator'): *http://arealvalidator.com/*
- World Wide Web Consortium: *http://www.w3c.org/*

Section 2: General notes

(a) *Purposes.* The following checklist may be used as a basis for accessibility and related standards auditing, for either conventional web pages or more complex systems, such as VLEs.

(b) *Exceptions.* Some authenticated systems (e.g. VLEs) may not be 'read' by some online validator tools; these should be assessed manually, according to relevant guidelines.

(c) *To view* the HTML/XHTML of a web resource in Internet Explorer:

1. Open the web page.
2. Go to the 'View' menu.
3. Select 'Source'.

However, if the web page is in a frame:

1. Click the *right* mouse button over the page.
2. Select 'View Source'.

Similar methods may be used to view source-code on other web browsers.

(d) *Fixing problems* in conventional web pages will be possible using a web editor, such as Dreamweaver, either using the word processor interface or the source code view.

(e) *VLEs and other complex web-based systems* display output to the browser in normal HTML/XHTML mark-up, and therefore mark-up standards discussed below still apply; however, the mark-up displayed on the user's client computer is not usually an HTML document, but is generated by complex programs, i.e. you cannot simply open the VLE interface in a web editor such as Dreamweaver. Changing the HTML/XHTML output of a VLE will require modifying the underlying program that generates the mark-up. Suggestions for accessibility 'fixes' in complex systems, such as VLEs, should be passed to the relevant system company. Fixes may be possible by an experienced programmer in an 'open source' or similar context where the legal right to modify code is available. If a VLE is not 'open source' (e.g. commercial), editing the code could be in breach of copyright or your software licence. The bottom line is that you can still audit the web display of a VLE, but fixing the underlying code is usually necessary by the software developer.

(f) *Consistency*. Obviously, checking for standards is a global issue across web resources and institutional systems. Auditing only the initial 'homepage' in a conventional website will not ensure the entire site is accessible.

Section 3: Standards compliance

It is important to ensure web-based resources comply with W3C standards, for mark-up (e.g. HTML 4.01) and CSS.

Mark-up

Before checking for accessibility standards, you should make sure the resource complies with mark-up standards; there are several HTML-based mark-up specifications, each identified by 'doctype', e.g. the doctype for XHTML 1.1:

> <!DOCTYPE html PUBLIC "-//W3C//DTD XHTML 1.1//EN"
> "http://www.w3.org/TR/xhtml11/DTD/xhtml11.dtd">

Each mark-up standard has a distinct code base; briefly summarised, these are:

- *HTML 4.01.* An early, but still current mark-up standard, allowing for page layout (e.g. <font face="arial">), and frames. HTML 4.01

may be used to create accessible web pages, although use of WCAG accessibility standards rules out many otherwise standard features of HTML.

- *XHTML 1.0.* In three forms: Strict, Transitional and Frameset (for frames support); this version of XHTML has some layout support, but relies more on external CSS for layout and appearance.
- *XHTML 1.1.* The latest version of XHTML, almost entirely without support for layout mark-up, relying on CSS for document appearance. XHTML 1.1 is probably the best standard for accessibility support, including intrinsic requirement for some WCAG features, removal of element attributes for a more content-focused document and requirement to use only single documents (i.e. without frames support).
- *XHTML Basic.* A more flexible version of XHTML for support on mobile devices (e.g. PDAs).

For doctype information and detailed specifications on the latest mark-up standards, including older and draft (not yet standard) doctypes, see: *http://www.w3.org/MarkUp/*.

If you are developing conventional web pages using an editor such as Dreamweaver, you should choose the most appropriate mark-up standard to use in your resource; web editing software often uses a default mark-up standard, but this may usually be overridden in the application preferences, or by 'converting' the current document to an alternative standard (e.g. Dreamweaver allows for easy conversion of HTML to XHTML). However, you should also check the HEAD of your mark-up to make sure the desired standard is declared, editing this if required using the specifications provided at the W3C mark-up site.

Obviously, auditing complex resources, such as a commercial VLE, will normally entail passing recommendations for fixes to the software company.

Mark-up auditing

Checking a web resource using a W3C validator will reveal any mark-up errors or problems for the current declared doctype (e.g. XHTML 1.1). Additionally, if no doctype is present (i.e. missing from the document HEAD), validation will usually not take place. The range of errors that may arise will also depend on the doctype you have declared in the resource HEAD; e.g. if you include <font face="arial"> in your HTML

4.01 document, this will not cause errors, but this mark-up will cause a warning for a doctype that does not support this particular element, such as XHTML 1.1.

Methods of auditing mark-up include:

- by manually reviewing output code – see the relevant mark-up specifications at: *http://www.w3.org/MarkUp/*
- by automatic checking using the W3C online mark-up validator: *http://validator.w3.org/*

  ... or the alternative online 'Web Design Group' validator (this tool supports checking multiple files – up to 40 at a time – via a 'batch' option): *http://validator.aulinx.de/wdg-html-validator/*
- see also 'A real validator', a Windows application developed by the Web Design Group; this application is shareware (requires a fee) and supports XHTML if you follow the instructions on the website: *http://arealvalidator.com/*

Once you are satisfied your mark-up is valid, or have viewed validation notification on a W3C validator, you may add an appropriate W3C image to your page.

Pre-existing code is available to include this logo on your page, including a hyperlink for users actually to check your page at the W3C mark-up site. For valid mark-up logos, see: *http://www.w3.org/WAI/WCAG1-Conformance.html.*

CSS validator

The W3C site also includes a CSS validator for auditing CSS used for document layout. CSS files have a .css extension and the CSS code refers to mark-up elements (and attributes), e.g. a simple CSS rule to format the <p> paragraph tag to display as blue:

P: {color: #0000ff};

There are currently two types of CSS, level 1 and level 2, the latter offering somewhat more complex layout support. CSS files are linked to HTML-based documents in the HEAD region of the mark-up file, e.g.:

<link rel="stylesheet" href="../mystyle.css" type="text/css"/>

Detailed specifications defining CSS are available at the W3C site:

- CSS Level 1: *http://www.w3.org/TR/REC-CSS1/*
- CSS Level 2: *http://www.w3.org/TR/REC-CSS2/*

The online CSS validator is located at: *http://jigsaw.w3.org/css-validator/*

To check your CSS file(s) are valid, you can:

- upload the CSS file(s) on the validator page;
- copy and paste your CSS code into a text-box on the CSS validator page ('Validate by Direct Input');
- supply the URL of the web page containing CSS links ('Validate by URI');
- supply the URL of the CSS file itself (also 'Validate by URI').

When you are happy you have met CSS standards, you will be able to display a CSS validation logo (available from the online validation results page).

Section 4: Web Content Accessibility Guidelines 1.0

Once your mark-up and CSS are compliant with W3C standards, you should audit your web resource for accessibility compliance. The W3C's 'Web Accessibility Initiative' (WAI) provides the 'Web Content Accessibility Guidelines' (WCAG), defining standards for accessible web resources. The full WCAG document is available at: *http://www.w3.org/TR/WAI-WEBCONTENT/*.

There are three levels of compliance defined by the guidelines, priority 1, priority 2 and priority 3. Compliance with priority 1 entitles the Web resource to 'A'; compliance with priorities 1 and 2 allows 'AA' and compliance with priorities 1, 2 and 3 allows 'AAA'. The relationship between the 'priorities' and 'guidelines' are defined on the WCAG site (2004):

Conformance Level "A": all priority 1 checkpoints are satisfied;

Conformance Level "Double-A": all priority 1 and 2 checkpoints are satisfied;

Conformance Level "Triple-A": all priority 1, 2 and 3 checkpoints are satisfied ...

The WCAG site (2004) defines the priorities as follows:

Priority 1: A web content developer must satisfy this checkpoint. Otherwise, one or more groups will find it impossible to access information in the document. Satisfying this checkpoint is a basic requirement for some groups to be able to use web documents.

Priority 2: A web content developer should satisfy this checkpoint. Otherwise, one or more groups will find it difficult to access information in the document. Satisfying this checkpoint will remove significant barriers to accessing web documents.

Priority 3: A web content developer may address this checkpoint. Otherwise, one or more groups will find it somewhat difficult to access information in the document. Satisfying this checkpoint will improve access to web documents.

There are 14 WCAG guidelines, each contains several 'checkpoints'; checkpoints are also defined according to a priority level, e.g. a checkpoint under Guideline 3 is: '3.3 Use style sheets to control layout and presentation'. This checkpoint is also defined as 'priority 2'.

To make it easier to view the requirements of each priority, this appendix displays all the checkpoints arranged by priority, rather than by guideline. To view the original arrangement, see the WCAG site: *http://www.w3.org/TR/WAI-WEBCONTENT/*. Note some checkpoints apply to several Priorities under certain circumstances (for a quick view of checkpoints with these circumstances indicated and arranged by Priority level, see *http://www.w3.org/TR/WCAG10/full-checklist .html*).

The guidelines define issues for web accessibility under 14 distinct categories, these are defined on the WCAG site as follows:

1. Provide equivalent alternatives to auditory and visual content.

2. Do not rely on colour alone.

3. Use mark-up and style sheets and do so properly.

4. Clarify natural language usage.

5. Create tables that transform gracefully.

6. Ensure that pages featuring new technologies transform gracefully.

7. Ensure user control of time-sensitive content changes.

8. Ensure direct accessibility of embedded user interfaces.

9. Design for device-independence.

10. Use interim solutions.

11. Use W3C technologies and guidelines.

12. Provide context and orientation information.

13. Provide clear navigation mechanisms.

14. Ensure that documents are clear and simple.

The checkpoints are displayed in the following pages, arranged by priority level.

Methods for interpreting and using the checkpoints include:

■ Detailed examples illustrating the checkpoints ('techniques for checkpoint') may be found at: *http://www.w3.org/TR/WCAG10 -HTML-TECHS/*.

■ Search for further examples on the W3C site (*http://www.w3c.org*) using the site search box to look up the required mark-up element name (e.g. 'alt').

■ For automated WCAG auditing, see Sections 5 and 6 later in this appendix.

■ Although the information below is cited without changes from the WCAG site, I have included a few additional notes (indicated by an asterisk).

■ For references to other guides indicated in the following tables, see the original WCAG document at: *http://www.w3.org/TR/WAI -WEBCONTENT/*.

■ WCAG logos: see the WCAG site for images that you can display on your pages if they meet one of the three priority levels (A, AA, AAA): *http://www.w3.org/TR/WAI-WEBCONTENT/*.

Copyright Information on the WCAG:

Web Content Accessibility Guidelines 1.0
W3C Recommendation 5-May-1999

This version:

http://www.w3.org/TR/1999/WAI-WEBCONTENT-19990505

(plain text, PostScript, PDF, gzip tar file of HTML, zip archive of HTML)

Latest version:

http://www.w3.org/TR/WAI-WEBCONTENT

Previous version:

http://www.w3.org/TR/1999/WAI-WEBCONTENT-19990324

Editors:

Wendy Chisholm, Trace R & D Center, University of Wisconsin – Madison

Gregg Vanderheiden, Trace R & D Center, University of Wisconsin – Madison

Ian Jacobs, W3C.

Priority 1

Checklist item	Checkpoint notes
1.1. Provide a text equivalent for every non-text element (e.g. via 'alt', 'longdesc' or in element content). This includes: images, graphical representations of text (including symbols), image map regions, animations (e.g. animated GIFs), applets and programmatic objects, ASCII art, frames, scripts, images used as list bullets, spacers, graphical buttons, sounds (played with or without user interaction), stand-alone audio files, audio tracks of video and video.	For example, in HTML use 'alt' for the IMG, INPUT and APPLET elements, or provide a text equivalent in the content of the OBJECT and APPLET elements. For complex content (e.g. a chart) where the 'alt' text does not provide a complete text equivalent, provide an additional description using, for example, 'longdesc' with IMG or FRAME, a link inside an OBJECT element or a description link. For image maps, either use the 'alt' attribute with AREA, or use the MAP element with A elements (and other text) as content. Refer also to checkpoints 9.1 and 13.10.
1.2. Provide redundant text links for each active region of a server-side image map.	Refer also to checkpoints 1.5 and 9.1. *See section '7.4.4 Server-side image maps' in the WCAG techniques at: *http://www.w3.org/TR/WCAG10 -HTML-TECHS/*.

Table (*cont'd*)

Checklist item	Checkpoint notes
1.3. Until user agents can automatically read aloud the text equivalent of a visual track, provide an auditory description of the important information of the visual track of a multimedia presentation.	Synchronize the auditory description with the audio track as per checkpoint 1.4. Refer to checkpoint 1.1 for information about textual equivalents for visual information.
1.4. For any time-based multimedia presentation (e.g. a movie or animation), synchronise equivalent alternatives (e.g. captions or auditory descriptions of the visual track) with the presentation.	*Multimedia files such as Flash allow for 'captions' to display text alternatives when displaying audio or video; these captions may be useful for deaf/hard-of-hearing users.
2.1. Ensure that all information conveyed with colour is also available without colour, for example from context or mark-up.	*It is unwise to rely on colour to convey information (e.g. an important notice displayed in red will not convey importance for blind users); this should be indicated in <B> (bold) or <strong>, or should be indicated in plain language in the context of the text.
4.1. Clearly identify changes in the natural language of a document's text and any text equivalents (e.g. captions).	For example, in HTML use the 'lang' attribute. In XML, use 'xml:lang'.
5.1. For data tables, identify row and column headers.	For example, in HTML use TD to identify data cells and TH to identify headers.
5.2. For data tables that have two or more logical levels of row or column headers, use mark-up to associate data cells and header cells.	For example, in HTML use THEAD, TFOOT and TBODY to group rows, COL and COLGROUP to group columns, and the 'axis', 'scope', and 'headers' attributes to describe more complex relationships among data.
6.1. Organize documents so they may be read without style sheets. For example, when an HTML document is rendered without associated style	When content is organised logically, it will be rendered in a meaningful order when style sheets are turned off or not supported.

Table (*cont'd*)

sheets, it must still be possible to read the document.	
6.2. Ensure that equivalents for dynamic content are updated when the dynamic content changes.	*See section '8.1' in the WCAG techniques at: *http://www.w3.org/TR/ WCAG10-HTML-TECHS/*.
6.3. Ensure that pages are usable when scripts, applets or other programmatic objects are turned off or not supported. If this is not possible, provide equivalent information on an alternative accessible page.	For example, ensure that links that trigger scripts work when scripts are turned off or not supported (e.g. do not use 'javascript:' as the link target). If it is not possible to make the page usable without scripts, provide a text equivalent with the NOSCRIPT element, use a server-side script instead of a client-side script or provide an alternative accessible page as per checkpoint 11.4. Refer also to guideline 1.
7.1. Until user agents allow users to control flickering, avoid causing the screen to flicker.	*Note*: People with photosensitive epilepsy can have seizures triggered by flickering or flashing in the 4–59 flashes per second (Htz) range with a peak sensitivity at 20 Htz as well as quick changes from dark to light (like strobe lights).
8.1. Make programmatic elements such as scripts and applets directly accessible or compatible with assistive technologies	Refer also to guideline 6. *See section '8.2' in the WCAG techniques at: *http://www.w3.org/TR/ WCAG10-HTML-TECHS/*.
9.1. Provide client-side image maps instead of server-side image maps except where the regions cannot be defined with an available geometric shape.	Refer also to checkpoints 1.1, 1.2 and 1.5. *See section '7.4.3' in the WCAG techniques at: *http://www.w3.org/ TR/WCAG10-HTML-TECHS/*.
11.4. If, after your best efforts, you cannot create an accessible page, provide a link to an alternative page that uses W3C technologies, is accessible, has equivalent information (or functionality) and is updated as often as the inaccessible (original) page.	*For example, provide a static HTML alternative if you cannot make a script-generated page accessible. It may be necessary to update the alternative page manually to ensure content is complementary to the script-generated page.

Table (*cont'd*)

Checklist item	Checkpoint notes
12.1. Title each frame to facilitate frame identification and navigation.	For example, in HTML use the 'title' attribute on FRAME elements.
14.1. Use the clearest and simplest language appropriate for a site's content.	*Use concise language for navigation/menus, with hyperlink labels describing the content of actual resources as closely as possible.

Priority 2

Checklist item	Checkpoint notes
2.2. Ensure that foreground and background colour combinations provide sufficient contrast when viewed by someone having colour deficits or when viewed on a black-and-white screen.	*See section '7.5' in the WCAG techniques at: *http://www.w3.org/TR/WCAG10-HTML-TECHS/*.
3.1. When an appropriate mark-up language exists, use mark-up rather than images to convey information.	For example, use MathML to mark up mathematical equations, and style sheets to format text and control layout. Also, avoid using images to represent text – use text and style sheets instead. Refer also to guidelines 6 and 11.
3.2. Create documents that validate to published formal grammars.	For example, include a document type declaration at the beginning of a document that refers to a published DTD (e.g. the strict HTML 4.0 DTD).
3.3. Use style sheets to control layout and presentation.	For example, use the CSS 'font' property instead of the HTML FONT element to control font styles.
3.4. Use relative rather than absolute units in mark-up language attribute values and style-sheet property values.	For example, in CSS use 'em' or percentage lengths rather than 'pt' or 'cm', which are absolute units. If absolute units are used, validate that the rendered content is usable (refer to the section on validation).

Table (*cont'd*)

3.5. Use header elements to convey document structure and use them according to specification.	For example, in HTML use H2 to indicate a subsection of H1. Do not use headers for font effects.
3.6. Mark up lists and list items properly.	For example, in HTML nest OL, UL, and DL lists properly.
3.7. Mark up quotations. Do not use quotation mark-up for formatting effects such as indentation.	For example, in HTML use the Q and BLOCKQUOTE elements to mark-up short and longer quotations, respectively.
5.3. Do not use tables for layout unless the table makes sense when linearised. Otherwise, if the table does not make sense, provide an alternative equivalent (which may be a linearised version).	*Note*: Once user agents support style-sheet positioning, tables should not be used for layout. Refer also to checkpoint 3.3.
5.4. If a table is used for layout, do not use any structural mark-up for the purpose of visual formatting.	For example, in HTML do not use the TH element to cause the content of a (non-table header) cell to be displayed centred and in bold.
6.4. For scripts and applets, ensure that event handlers are input device-independent.	Refer to the definition of device-independence. *See section '8.2' in the WCAG techniques at: *http://www.w3.org/TR/WCAG10-HTML-TECHS/*
6.5. Ensure that dynamic content is accessible or provide an alternative presentation or page.	For example, in HTML use NOFRAMES at the end of each frameset. For some applications, server-side scripts may be more accessible than client-side scripts.
7.2. Until user agents allow users to control blinking, avoid causing content to blink (i.e. change presentation at a regular rate, such as turning on and off).	*See section: '8.2' in the WCAG techniques at: *http://www.w3.org/TR/WCAG10-HTML-TECHS/*.
7.3. Until user agents allow users to freeze moving content, avoid movement in pages.	When a page includes moving content, provide a mechanism within a script or applet to allow users to freeze motion or updates. Using style

Table (*cont'd*)

Checklist item	Checkpoint notes
	sheets with scripting to create movement allows users to turn off or override the effect more easily. Refer also to guideline 8.
7.4. Until user agents provide the ability to stop the refresh, do not create periodically auto-refreshing pages.	For example, in HTML do not cause pages to auto-refresh with 'HTTP-EQUIV=refresh' until user agents allow users to turn off the feature.
7.5. Until user agents provide the ability to stop auto-redirect, do not use mark-up to redirect pages automatically. Instead, configure the server to perform redirects.	*See section '12.6' in the WCAG techniques at: *http://www.w3.org/ TR/WCAG10HTML-TECHS/*.
8.1. Make programmatic elements such as scripts and applets directly accessible or compatible with assistive technologies	Refer also to guideline 6. *See section '12.4' in the WCAG techniques at: *http://www.w3 .org/TR/WCAG10-HTM-TECHS/*.
9.2. Ensure that any element that has its own interface can be operated in a device-independent manner.	Refer to the definition of device independence. Refer also to guideline 8. *See section: '8.2' in the WCAG techniques at: *http://www.w3.org/ TR/WCAG10-HTML-TECHS/*
9.3. For scripts, specify logical event handlers rather than device-dependent event handlers.	*See section '12.4' in the WCAG techniques at: *http://www.w3.org/ TR/WCAG10-HTML-TECHS/*.
10.1. Until user agents allow users to turn off spawned windows, do not cause pop-ups or other windows to appear and do not change the current window without informing the user.	For example, in HTML avoid using a frame whose target is a new window.
10.2. Until user agents support explicit associations between labels and form controls, for all form controls with implicitly associated labels, ensure that the label is properly positioned.	The label must immediately precede its control on the same line (allowing more than one control/label per line) or be in the line preceding the control (with only one label and one control per line). Refer also to checkpoint 12.4.

Table (*cont'd*)

11.1. Use W3C technologies when they are available and appropriate for a task and use the latest versions when supported.	Refer to the list of references for information about where to find the latest W3C specifications and [WAI-UA-SUPPORT] for information about user agent support for W3C technologies.
11.2. Avoid deprecated features of W3C technologies.	For example, in HTML do not use the deprecated FONT element; use style sheets instead (e.g. the 'font' property in CSS).
12.2. Describe the purpose of frames and how frames relate to each other if it is not obvious by frame titles alone.	For example, in HTML, use 'longdesc', or a description link.
12.3. Divide large blocks of information into more manageable groups where natural and appropriate to do so.	For example, in HTML use OPTGROUP to group OPTION elements inside a SELECT; group form controls with FIELDSET and LEGEND; use nested lists where appropriate; use headings to structure documents, etc. Refer also to guideline 3.
12.4. Associate labels explicitly with their controls.	For example, in HTML use LABEL and its 'for' attribute.
13.1. Clearly identify the target of each link.	Link text should be meaningful enough to make sense when read out of context – either on its own or as part of a sequence of links. Link text should also be terse. For example, in HTML write 'Information about version 4.3' instead of 'click here'. In addition to clear link text, content developers may further clarify the target of a link with an informative link title (e.g. in HTML the 'title' attribute).
13.2. Provide metadata to add semantic information to pages and sites.	For example, use RDF to indicate the document's author, the type of content, etc. *Note*: Some HTML user agents can build navigation tools from document relations described

Table (*cont'd*)

Checklist item	Checkpoint notes
	by the HTML LINK element and 'rel' or 'rev' attributes (e.g. rel='next', rel='previous', rel='index', etc.). Refer also to checkpoint 13.5.
13.3. Provide information about the general layout of a site (e.g. a site map or table of contents).	In describing site layout, highlight and explain available accessibility features.
13.4. Use navigation mechanisms in a consistent manner.	*Top-level navigation options (i.e. main categories as opposed to sub-categories) should ideally remain the same across all documents, providing a consistent method to navigate.

Priority 3

Checklist item	Checkpoint notes
1.5. Until user agents render text equivalents for client-side image map links, provide redundant text links for each active region of a client-side image map.	Refer also to checkpoints 1.2 and 9.1. *See section '7.4.2' in the WCAG techniques at: *http://www.w3.org/TR/WCAG10-HTML-TECHS/*.
2.2. Ensure that foreground and background colour combinations provide sufficient contrast when viewed by someone having colour deficits or when viewed on a black-and-white screen.	Refer also to checkpoints 1.2 and 9.1. *See section: '7.5' in the WCAG techniques at: *http://www.w3.org/TR/WCAG10-HTML-TECHS/*.
4.2. Specify the expansion of each abbreviation or acronym in a document on first occurrence.	For example, in HTML use the 'title' attribute of the ABBR and ACRONYM elements. Providing the expansion in the main body of the document also helps document usability.

Table (*cont'd*)

4.3. Identify the primary natural language of a document.	For example, in HTML set the 'lang' attribute on the HTML element. In XML, use 'xml:lang'. Server operators should configure servers to take advantage of HTTP content negotiation mechanisms.
5.5. Provide summaries for tables.	For example, in HTML use the 'summary' attribute of the TABLE element.
5.6. Provide abbreviations for header labels.	For example, in HTML use the 'abbr' attribute on the TH element.
9.4. Create a logical tab order through links, form controls and objects.	For example, in HTML specify tab order via the 'tabindex' attribute or ensure a logical page design.
9.5. Provide keyboard shortcuts to important links (including those in client-side image maps), form controls and groups of form controls.	For example, in HTML specify shortcuts via the 'accesskey' attribute.
10.3. Until user agents (including assistive technologies) render side-by-side text correctly, provide a linear text alternative (on the current page or some other) for all tables that lay out text in parallel, word-wrapped columns.	*Note*: Please consult the definition of linearised table. This checkpoint benefits people with user agents (such as some screen readers) that are unable to handle blocks of text presented side by side; the checkpoint should not discourage content developers from using tables to represent tabular information.
10.4. Until user agents handle empty controls correctly, include default, place-holding characters in edit boxes and text areas.	For example, in HTML do this for TEXTAREA and INPUT.
10.5. Until user agents (including assistive technologies) render adjacent links distinctly, include non-link, printable characters (surrounded by spaces) between adjacent links.	*See section '6.2' in the WCAG techniques at: *http://www.w3.org/ TR/WCAG10-HTML-TECHS/*.

Table (*cont'd*)

Checklist item	Checkpoint notes
11.3. Provide information so that users may receive documents according to their preferences (language, content type, etc.).	*Note*: Use content negotiation where possible. *Provide alternative formats, e.g. where a Word file is used, also provide an alternative HTML version.
13.5. Provide navigation bars to highlight and give access to the navigation mechanism.	Provide information so that users may receive documents *Use a menu of links to provide consistent navigation across all pages.
13.6. Group related links, identify the group (for user agents) and, until user agents do so, provide a way to bypass the group.	*See section '6.2' in the WCAG techniques at: *http://www.w3.org/TR/WCAG10-HTML-TECHS/*.
13.7. If search functions are provided, enable different types of searches for different skill levels and preferences.	*For example, provide an 'advanced' option for website search engines.
13.8. Place distinguishing information at the beginning of headings, paragraphs, lists, etc.	*Note*: This is commonly referred to as 'front-loading' and is especially helpful for people accessing information with serial devices such as speech synthesisers.
13.9. Provide information about document collections (i.e. documents comprising multiple pages).	For example, in HTML specify document collections with the LINK element and the 'rel' and 'rev' attributes. Another way to create a collection is by building an archive (with zip, tar and gzip, stuffit, etc.) of the multiple ages. *Note*: The performance improvement gained by offline processing can make browsing much less expensive for people with disabilities who may be browsing slowly.
13.10. Provide a means to skip over multiline ASCII art.	Refer to checkpoint 1.1 and the example of ASCII art in the glossary. *See section '7.3' in the WCAG techniques at: *http://www.w3.org/TR/WCAG10-HTML-TECHS/*.

Table (*cont'd*)

14.2. Supplement text with graphic or auditory presentations where they will facilitate comprehension of the page.	Refer also to guideline 1.
14.3. Create a style of presentation that is consistent across pages.	*Do not change the font size or layout style across a website but ensure style is consistent across all pages (i.e. using CSS).

Section 5: Bobby accessibility validation

The Bobby accessibility validator is probably the most popular tool for auditing WCAG compliance, and also allows for checking US 508 support (*http://www.section508.gov/*). Bobby is available in two forms: a commercial application, which may run on the Windows operating system, or an online tool, which restricts access to one document audit per minute. The URL for the application and online validator is: *http://bobby.watchfire.com*. The Bobby tool (online and application version) provides a detailed report of WCAG or US 508 complaince within an audited resource; additionally, 'repair' information and contextual examples of valid mark-up are also provided for 'warnings'. Bobby also provides its own logos for 'A', 'AA' or 'AAA'.

Section 6. Other validation methods

A range of further tools and approaches exist for accessibility auditing in web resources. An alternative to the commercial Bobby tool is 'A-prompt', a not-for-profit application developed at the University of Toronto (*http://aprompt.snow.utoronto.ca/*). A-prompt provides a slightly different interface than Bobby, requiring a step-by-step approach for assessing and 'repairing' resources, although a report may be viewed for later 'repairing'.

Further accessibility tools are available at the W3C accessibility resources site (*http://www.w3.org/WAI/ER/existingtools.htm*). The W3C also makes a range of further recommendations for accessibility compliance (Web Content Accessibility Guidelines 1.0: *http://www.w3 .org/TR/WAI-WEBCONTENT/*):

- Begin using validation methods at the earliest stages of development. Accessibility issues identified early are easier to correct and avoid.
- Use an automated accessibility tool and browser validation tool. Please note that software tools do not address all accessibility issues, such as the meaningfulness of link text, the applicability of a text equivalent, etc.
- Validate syntax (HTML, XML, etc.).
- Validate style sheets (e.g. CSS).
- Use a text-only browser or emulator (e.g. Lynx: *http://www.lynx .browser.org/*).
- Use multiple graphic browsers, with:
  - sounds and graphics loaded,
  - graphics not loaded,
  - sounds not loaded,
  - no mouse,
  - frames, scripts, style sheets and applets not loaded.
- Use several browsers, old and new.
- Use a self-voicing browser, a screen reader, magnification software, a small display (including a range of screen resolution settings, including 800 × 600 pixels per inch and higher resolutions), etc.
- Use spell and grammar checkers. A person reading a page with a speech synthesizer may not be able to decipher the synthesizer's best guess for a word with a spelling error. Eliminating grammar problems increases comprehension.
- Review the document for clarity and simplicity. Readability statistics, such as those generated by some word processors, may be useful indicators of clarity and simplicity. Better still, ask an experienced (human) editor to review written content for clarity. Editors can also improve the usability of documents by identifying potentially sensitive cultural issues that might arise due to language or icon usage.
- Invite people with disabilities to review documents. Expert and novice users with disabilities will provide valuable feedback about accessibility or usability problems and their severity.

Additionally, it is worth remembering that WCAG and other W3C standards are closely aligned, so that mark-up compliance (e.g. XHTML 1.1) will ensure some accessibility support in compliant browsing software or other user 'agents' (e.g. screen readers). Several additional resources are available for checking WCAG:

- General index of resources for web accessibility: *http://www.w3.org/WAI/*

- A PowerPoint presentation introducing web accessibility standards: *http://www.w3.org/Talks/WAI-Intro/slide1-0.html*

- A checklist of key aspects for implementing WCAG: *http://www.w3.org/TR/WAI-WEBCONTENT/full-checklist.html*

- A self-evaluation checklist for WCAG: *http://www.w3.org/WAI/eval/*

- The US 508 guidelines is another international accessibility standard, closely aligned with WCAG. These guidelines are legal requirements for federal (government/public body) web resources in the US. The main 508 site is located at: *http://www.section508.gov/*. A guide to the 508 regulations is located at: *http://www.access-board.gov/sec508/guide/1194.22.htm*

Glossary of terms

Note: If you are looking for a URL (web address), see also Appendix 1, E-learning online (selected URLs).

Other glossaries:

- JISC Glossary (mainly HE acronyms and Educational Technology terms): *http://www.jisc.ac.uk/index.cfm?name=about_glossary*
- FOLDOC Online Computing Dictionary: *http://wombat.doc.ic.ac.uk/foldoc/index.html*

Academy (higher education academy). This body provides advocacy and support for activities in the HE sector.

Accessibility. Accessibility on the Web relates to ensuring computer systems can be used effectively by people possessing various kinds of disability. See also WCAG, Usability.

Active directory. A Microsoft standard for storing profiles, i.e. user accounts on a network. See also Directory.

Address bar. The text box in a Web browser where a URL may be entered for Web browsing. See also URL.

Adobe Acrobat document. See PDF.

ADSL (Asymmetric Digital Subscriber Line). A standard for fast broadband internet access. See also Broadband.

API (application programming interface). Provides a method for customising software, typically via a command-line interface supplied as an internal system feature. An API could be used to develop system extensions or add-ons, or for integration with other systems.

Archie. See FTP.

ARPANET. The first network to allow communication between remote sites, an early forerunner of the modern Internet. See also Internet.

ASCII. (American standard code for information interchange). The basic text format used by computer systems, also called 'plain text'.

ASP. (active server pages). A Microsoft technology allowing for interactive and database-driven web content.

Assistive technology. Equipment used to access web and other digital resources for disabled users. See also Braille reader, Screen reader, WCAG, WAI.

Asynchronous. In IT, this indicates a form of communication that depends on the exchange of messages or other information over a period of time, but not necessarily in the same session. E-mail is a form of asynchronous communication. See also Synchronous.

Authentication. A computing term to describe the verification of information, e.g. a login password. See also LDAP, Directory.

Authority file. A list of standard terms that may be used to restrict data entry to defined categories or descriptions.

AVI (Audio Video Interleave). A Microsoft video and audio format providing good file size compression.

Backup. The process of storing copies of files in the event of data loss.

Bespoke. A term used in IT to describe customisation of systems or software.

Binary files. Unlike 'plain text' or ASCII, binary files are not readable by humans, but consist of bits (1s and 0s), which comprise machine code; binary files are often used by proprietary applications for document formats such as Word or PowerPoint. See also ASCII.

BITNET (because it's time network). An early US-based academic and research computer network, superseded by CREN, the Corporation for Research and Educational Networking (US). See also CREN, JANET.

Blended learning/distributed learning. The use of several forms of teaching delivery. In the context of e-learning, this might indicate a combination of class-based contact and remote communication via e-mail. See also Distance learning.

BMP (bitmap). An image format that provides high PPI (pixels per inch) resolution but uses lots of disk space.

Braille reader. A form of assistive technology to display digital text dynamically in the form of raised Braille characters. See also Assistive technology.

Broadband. A faster method of connecting to the Internet for smaller organisations and home users. Examples of broadband technology include ISDN (integrated services digital network) and ADSL (asymmetric digital subscriber line); broadband Internet access is many times the speed of a modem, allowing for delivery of content-rich media and video. Although broadband is becoming increasingly popular, it is still overshadowed by the cheaper and more popular modem method of accessing the Internet. See also Modem.

CD-ROM. A removable disk that can typically store up to 700 megabytes of computer data. The emergence of CD-ROM has allowed for the wider distribution of computer software and other data, traditionally limited to the 1.4 megabytes of the 3.5-inch floppy disk; CD-ROM stands for 'compact disk read only memory'; more recently, CD-R (recordable) and CD-RW (re-writeable) forms have become popular.

CETIS (Centre for Educational Technology Interoperability Standards). This JISC-funded group provides advocacy and discussion on interoperability standards in educational technology, including the IMS, SCORM and other e-learning standards. See also Learning object.

CGI (common gateway interface). A method to execute (run) applications on a remote server, based on actions on a user's computer (typically via a web browser). Examples of CGI applications include online purchasing systems and web feedback forms, where messages are directed by the remote CGI program to an e-mail server for delivery to a recipient e-mail address.

CILIP (Chartered Institute of Library and Information Professionals). Arguably the foremost professional body for the information sector in the UK, providing advocacy and support for information professionals working in higher education, health, further education, statutory education, information science and many related fields.

Client. A networking term used to describe a user terminal or access point within a network; for example, a student's networked PC is a client within the network, as opposed to the 'server' providing network resources. Software used on the end-user computer is also called 'client software'. See also TCP, IP and Server.

CMS. See Content management system.

Codec (coder/decoder). A small 'translator' file that enables audio or video files to play via multimedia software such as Windows Media Player; certain audio or video formats require a supporting codec to function (i.e. where the codec is not provided as standard with an operating system such as Windows).

Collaborative learning. The participation of several individuals in an educational activity; in a digital context, this often involves cooperative work using e-learning tools.

Content management system (CMS). A typically web-based system resembling a VLE, allowing users to upload and manage documents and other files; content management systems are often used to provide an easily updated website or internal Intranet.

CREN (Corporation for Research and Educational Net-working). A leading US network for academic and research organisations. See also BITNET.

CSS (cascading style sheets). A file containing script to define the style, colours and general appearance of web-based documents; CSS script is different from conventional HTML. See also W3C.

Directory. A computing term used to describe a collection of data. Directory services for user accounts on a network include Microsoft Active Directory and Novell NDS. This term also describes a 'folder' used to contain documents and other files within a larger directory hierarchy.

Distance learning. The delivery of education via communication facilities to a location typically remote from the provider. See also Blended learning.

Distributed learning. See Blended learning.

DIVX (digital video express). This video format provides very high levels of compression while retaining video quality.

E-learning (electronic learning). A term used to describe any form of IT in the context of education, but more popularly used to define learning delivered via the Internet and a web browser such as Internet Explorer. E-learning may also be considered a generic term, which may be applied either to learning technology itself, or to pedagogical methods in an online or electronic context.

E-mail. Invented during the early 1970s, e-mail comprises several fields allowing for the effective relay of messages across the Internet, including Sender, Recipient and Subject.

Firewall. An intermediary service between network services and the end user; the firewall may be used to limit the transmission of certain kinds of data and prevent direct access to server systems.

Flash. An interactive vector format (lines and filled shapes) developed by Macromedia; the Flash MX editing software is used to create Flash animations and interactive features; the free Flash player is required to run flash files (.swf) on the client computer.

Frames. A standard in HTML allowing for positioning of multiple windows containing distinct pages within the web browser. Frames have been popularly used to provide navigation features in the past, but the latest version of XHTML (1.1) has deprecated this feature, mainly due to lack of support in assistive technology.

FTP (file transmission protocol). A method to publish files on the Internet (via an FTP server); an FTP application such as Winsock FTP (*http://www.ipswitch.com*) is required to upload or download files remotely on an FTP server. FTP also describes the protocol used to transmit files via an FTP application. 'Archie' servers provide a method to search public FTP sites worldwide, traditionally using a command line telnet connection, although web versions are also available (e.g. *http://www.filewatcher.com*). See also Protocol.

GIF (graphical interchange format). Another popular and file-size-efficient image format, suitable for clip art and lower resolution images.

Gopher. An early document publishing and retrieval system developed by the University of Minnesota; Gopher systems have largely disappeared, supplanted by the World Wide Web.

GPRS (general packet radio service). A standard for transmission of radio (wireless) networking; GPRS is cited as a cheaper form of long-range Internet access for mobile devices (e.g. PDA), using a system in which the user pays for the volume of data sent or received only. Unlike WAP-based networks, GPRS allows for access of the conventional Internet via a mobile device. See also PDA, WAP, WiLAN.

Hardcopy. Printed or other paper-based documents.

Hardware. Computing equipment, such as a monitor or other 'physical' components.

HTML (hypertext mark-up language). HTML is a mark-up standard used to construct web documents. Typically, ordinary text is 'marked-up' using a range of 'tags' to define both the appearance of textual material and other descriptive information; 'word processing' of HTML (as opposed to manual editing) has become popular using web editors such as Dreamweaver and FrontPage, but knowledge of HTML and web standards is still important for the development of web-based systems. See also XHTML, W3C.

Hyperlink (hyper-text link). A link provided on a web page to another resource, including web documents, graphics or other resources. See also HTML, Mark-up.

ICQ ('I seek you'). A popular chat system. See also Synchronous.

IMS (instructional management system). IMS is a standard for packaging, describing and presenting electronic content in a reusable form compliant with a range of systems. IMS could be used to create a presentation containing multiple documents or an interactive quiz. See also Learning object.

Internet. Also called 'The Net'; Internet is the term given to describe the worldwide network of smaller networks, all able to send and receive information using common communications standards. Large organisations typically connect to the Internet directly via the telecommunications industry, but home users usually need to connect via a third-party such as an ISP (Internet service provider). See also Network, ISP, TCP, IP, LAN.

Internet search engine. A system for searching and retrieving web-based documents; popular search engines include Google and AltaVista. Owing to poor classification or descriptive standards on the World Wide Web, Internet searching is often inaccurate and imprecise. See also Metadata.

Internet service provider (ISP). A company providing Internet access for individual (mainly home) users. ISPs also provide e-mail, web hosting and other internet services for clients. Popular ISPs include BT Openworld and AOL.

Intranet. Typically, an internal information system available via the Web and protected from unauthorised access by authentication (i.e. username and password login).

IP address. The 'Internet protocol' address of an individual computer within a network; this is a numerical address (e.g. 168.192.0.1). See also TCP.

ISDN (integrated services digital network). See Broadband.

ISP. See Internet service provider.

JANET (Joint Academic Network). The UK academic network responsible for regulating and coordinating internet access for higher and further education.

Java. A programming language and standard for interactive content on the Web, Java applications may also function in a typical Windows environment (and on other operating systems); a Java plug-in (Java run-time environment) is required to use Java-based software. Java is developed and distributed by Sun Microsystems (*http://www.sun.com*). Although the Sun distribution of Java is used universally by web browsers, Microsoft Internet Explorer also provides an alternative system called the Microsoft Virtual Machine.

JavaScript. A programming language or script used to provide interactive features within web documents.

JISC (the Joint Information Systems Committee). JISC provides strategic advice on network and information technology for UK further and higher education organisations.

JPEG (joint photographic experts group). A high-resolution image format, suitable for digital photographs and other high-quality graphics.

Kilobyte (KB). A unit of memory or data size, 1 kilobyte represents 1024 bytes. See also Megabyte.

LAN (local area network). A network of computers within a defined area, providing shared printing and other services; the LAN may be self-sufficient, without links to the Internet. However an LAN may also be used provide Internet access to client computers. See also TCP, IP, WiLAN, Internet.

LDAP (lightweight directory authentication protocol). An authentication standard used to provide remote login verification against a directory service such as Active Directory. See also Directory, Protocol.

Learning object. The concept of the learning object considers an electronic document, presentation or interactive assessment as a 'packaged' resource, which can be created using learning object editors and published on compatible systems such as VLEs. See also IMS, SCORM.

LINUX (Linus Unix). A UNIX-based operating system; traditional versions of LINUX provided a text-only interface, but modern versions provide a Windows-style interface. See also UNIX.

Local area network. See LAN.

LTSN (The Learning and Teaching Support Network). This organisation supports a range of HE activities, via subject-focused support centres located across the UK.

Mark-up. A term used to describe the use of 'tags' to define the purpose of textual information. In HTML (hyper-text mark-up language) 'tags' enclose text to instruct the web browser how to display content; for example, <P>Hello</P> would display the text as a paragraph inline with other content on the page. The tags Hello would display the text in bold. Additionally, mark-up is composed of 'elements', e.g. <p> (for paragraph) and 'attributes', allowing for more precise definition, e.g. <p align="left">. Recent versions of HTML (i.e. XHTML) have seen a reduction in attributes and use of external cascading style sheet (CSS) files for document layout. Other recent mark-up standards such as XML (extensible mark-up language) are also used to define the semantic purpose of content for use within custom applications, e.g. <author>Paul Catherall</author>. See also XML, HTML, XHTML, CSS, W3C.

MathML. (mathematical mark-up language). A script based on XML, used to present mathematical equations; MathML may be used to display equations in a typical HTML-based document (providing an interpreter is present, such as a web-based VLE capable of displaying

MathML equations; MathML is not directly supported in typical web browsers). See also XML.

Megabyte (MB). A larger unit of file space or memory, representing 1024 kilobytes. See also Kilobyte.

Metadata. Metadata is the term used to describe classification, querying and retrieval methods for web-based resources. Metadata comprise both the descriptive format used to describe or categorise resources (e.g. Dublin Core, MARC) and the technology used to store information (e.g. HTML, XML). Some Internet search engines provide some support for meta information, contained in tags such as 'Description', 'Author', etc. An advanced standard for the Web (the Dublin Core) is also supported by some search engines. See also Internet search engines.

MIDI (musical instrument digital interface). This audio format produces a file-size-efficient output and will work on most operating systems.

MIS (managed information systems). Another term used to describe systems used by universities to store and manage central data, such as course information or course results. See also SRS.

MLE (managed learning environment). MLE is the term applied to a system providing a range of institutional facilities, typically accessed via a web browser. For example, the virtual learning environment (VLE) may form a part of an institution's MLE, but other MLE components could include a library management system (i.e. OPAC), or access to personal course records. See also VLE.

Modem (modulator/demodulator). A device used to establish a cheap but fairly slow connection to the Internet (with a maximum speed of 56 kilobits per second). See also Broadband.

Mosaic. An early popular web browser, developed by Marc Andreessen; Mosaic was the first web browser to allow for images.

MP3 (MPEG-1 audio layer 3). The most compact and popular digital audio format in use today; MP3 audio is now supported by Windows Media Player.

MPEG (Moving Picture Experts Group). An audio and video format providing high levels of compression and supported by Windows Media Player.

Network. The term used to describe a number of computers linked together, often sharing files and resources such as printers. Networks use world-standard technology to enable computers to 'speak' to one another, including a unique address for each networked computer (IP address) and a common communications medium (TCP or transmission control protocol). See also TCP, IP, LAN.

News feed. The method used for online publishing of a file containing news information. See also RSS, Newsgroups.

Newsgroups. An e-mail-based discussion and bulletin service, traditionally accessed using a special newsreader program to display and sort messages based on subject headings, e.g. 'sci.geology'. Newsgroups (also called Usenet) are still widely available on the Internet via web-based services such as Google Usenet (*http://groups.google.com*).

Novell Directory Services (NDS). A directory service based on the Novell Netware server. See also Directory, Active directory.

OCR (optical character recognition). Software often used with scanner equipment to analyse scanned images of text and convert these images to actual text documents.

Online learning. Synonymous with e-learning, this indicates more precisely forms of education delivery via the Internet or World Wide Web.

Online public access catalogue (OPAC). These systems traditionally provided a text interface (i.e. via telnet) to search or manage library management systems; modern OPACS are typically web or Windows based.

Open source. Generally indicates a computer program that may be downloaded and used without charge; some e-learning/VLE systems are open source.

Operating system (OS). The operating system is a system management application used to manage other compatible applications and computer hardware. The Windows, UNIX and Macintosh systems are examples of operating systems.

ORACLE. An industry-standard relational database management system (RDMS) for use within network applications.

Path. The location of a resource within a computer file system, either in the context of a local desktop computer (e.g. C:\Windows\my_file .doc), a local network (e.g. \\MyPC\docs\my_file.doc) or on the Internet (e.g. *http://www.someplace.com/file.doc*).

PC (personal computer). A term used to describe a standard of computer based on the Intel processor, originally developed by the IBM corporation in 1981; the main characteristics of IBM-compatible PCs were an internal hard drive, removable 'floppy disk' media and a standard BIOS (basic input/output system) used for system setup. Although much enhanced, the IBM-compatible model remains the prevalent architecture for computing.

PDF (portable document format). The Acrobat document format, consisting of vectors (lines and shapes); PDF files are highly compact, allowing for faster downloading via the Internet.

Perl. A programming language used with web-based systems, often to provide interactive content. See also CGI.

Personal computer. See PC.

Personal digital assistant (PDA). A small hand-held computer, providing a highly compact operating system, applications, communication features and mobile network access.

PINE (program for internet news & e-mail). An early text-based e-mail program popular on UNIX-based systems. See also UNIX.

Plug-in. A 'helper' application, used to view, play or otherwise access a proprietary format. See also Codec.

Portal. This term describes a web-based directory containing hyperlinks to online resources or the ability to search a collection of digital documents. This term is now also been used to describe the homepage or interface to an institutional website; a university portal may provide access to an e-learning system, a library catalogue (OPAC) or other online systems.

Protocol. The technical standard used to transmit data across a network. The TCP/IP protocol defines the transmission standard used for the Internet and local area networks. Other protocols include FTP and HTTP (hyper-text transfer protocol) for HTML documents. See also TCP, IP, FTP, Telnet, WAP, LDAP.

QuickTime. An audio and video standard developed for the Apple Macintosh computer system, but now available in other operating systems such as Windows. See also Codec.

RAID (redundant arrays of independent disks). A method to ensure data are available across several hard disk drives, preventing data loss.

RealAudio. An audio standard allowing for audio streaming; the RealPlayer application and plug-in is used to play the RealAudio format. See also Streaming.

RSS (rich site summary or really simple syndication). An XML-based document using the RDF metadata standard (resource description framework). RSS is used to deliver news items for viewing in a special RSS news reader or via a web-based reader. See also XML.

SCORM (sharable content object reference model). SCORM is a content packaging standard similar to IMS. See also learning objects.

Screen reader. A form of assistive technology for disabled uses, typically used to 'speak' or otherwise access digital resources such as web documents. See also assistive technology.

Search engine. See Internet search engine.

Server. Any networked computer providing network services, e.g. web services, FTP file services, e-mail or printing, typically via the TCP/IP protocols. See also Client, TCP, IP.

Single sign-on. A system allowing users to access multiple distinct online resources following only a single login.

SITS (strategic information technology services). A well-established student records system. See also SRS.

SMS (short messaging service). A short text message sent and received using mobile phones, pagers and integrated devices such as 'smart phones'.

SQL (structured query language). A popular relational database management system (RDMS) for storing network information, such as user records.

SRS (student records system). A term applied to a university system used to store and manage student records, including enrolment details. See also MIS.

Streaming. The technique is used to transmit audio or video files sequentially for user access, rather than download an entire file before 'running' the resource. See also RealAudio.

Synchronous. A form of communication in which messages or other information may be exchanged instantaneously. Chat programs are synchronous, because participants may respond to messages as soon as they appear on the screen. See also Asynchronous.

TCP (transmission control protocol). Together with the IP protocol, TCP regulates network transmission, using 'packets' to store and send data. A 'checksum' is used to compare packet sizes upon arrival at the destination client. See also IP, Client, Network.

Telnet. A text-based application used to log into Internet services; telnet is also the protocol used to transmit data in this context. Telnet is now less used as a user interface, being replaced by graphical and mouse-operated systems. See also Protocol.

UAAG (User Agent Accessibility Guidelines 1.0). These W3C guidelines are accessibility standards for the development of systems used to access web resources and are complementary to the WCAG accessibility standards for web resources. It is important that both web resources and systems used to access resources (user agents) comply with accessibility standards. UAAG applies to any system used to access the Web, including web browsers and assistive technology, such as Braille readers. See also Assistive technology, WCAG, W3C.

UNIX. An operating system capable of providing user access via telnet from a remote location; UNIX was developed in 1963 and remains an important system management environment. See also LINUX.

URL (universal resource locator). A web address, consisting of a protocol (e.g. 'http'/hyper-text transfer protocol), then a host or domain (e.g. 'somewhere.org') and a path to the desired resource on the server (e.g. '/docs/mydoc.htm'). URLs may use any of several protocols depending on the destination system (e.g. an FTP server would look like ftp://... whereas a web resource would look like http://...). See also Protocol, Path.

Usability. The ease with which users can interact with a typically web-based resource without extensive training. Usability is an important aspect in making web-based systems realistic media for the delivery of educational resources. See also Accessibility.

Usenet. See Newsgroups.

Virtual university/e-university. A term used to describe how electronic and Internet-based services can be deployed by libraries and institutions to provide a range of interactive facilities. See also Portal.

VLE (virtual learning environment). A term used to describe an education-focused resource publishing and communications system usually accessible via a web browser from any Internet-connected computer. Typically, VLEs require only minimal IT skills, allowing for relatively easy management of educational resources and sophisticated communication features, such as discussion boards for interaction between students and staff. See also E-learning, MLE.

WAP (wireless access protocol). A network transmission standard used to access the wireless internet, typically for long-range access using a WAP phone. WAP devices may browse WAP-enabled sites, but not ordinary websites. See also WML, GPRS, PDA, Protocol.

WAV (waveform). This audio format provides a high-quality output and is compatible with a wide range of operating systems.

Web accessibility initiative (WAI). A programme of activities developed by the W3C to promote and develop standards for accessibility and usability on the Web. See also W3C, WCAG, UAAG.

Web browser. A computer application used to access the World Wide Web; example web browsers include Netscape Navigator and Internet Explorer.

Web content accessibility guidelines (WCAG). A set of industry-standard guidelines for web accessibility, developed by the World Wide Web Consortium's WAI project. See also WAI, W3C.

Whiteboard. A presentation tool found in some e-learning systems, allowing tutors to draw pictures, type text and display presentations for students viewing the Whiteboard tool at the same time, but at a remote location.

Wireless local area network (WiLAN). A local area network providing connectivity via wireless technology, allowing for network services in any location within the radio signal field. See also LAN, GPRS, PDA, WAP.

Wireless mark up language (WML). A mark-up language similar to HTML, but based on XML, used to provide WAP-based documents. See also WAP.

World Wide Web. Web documents (HTML-based files) and supporting digital resources (such as images) are accessed via the Internet using a web browser installed on the user's computer. Using Internet technology, the World Wide Web, or Web for short, allows authors to publish and view documents according to range of recognised standards. See also HTML, XHTML, W3C, Internet.

World Wide Web Consortium (W3C). This is the most influential standards organisation coordinating the development of the World Wide Web; the W3C is chaired by the inventor of the Web, Tim Berners-Lee. See also CSS, HTML, XHTML, XML, WCAG, WAI, UAAG.

WYSIWYG (what you see is what you get). A concept in word processing software providing an interface to edit documents easily using windows, items, menus and pointers (WIMP), based around the idea that you can see the actual output or appearance of your document in the editor. Before WIMP/WYSIWYG standards, early word processors such as Mini Office required the user to 'mark-up' plain text using tags to indicate document appearance for printing (e.g. @Hello@ might print as **Hello**). WYSIWYG concepts have led to word processors such as Microsoft Word and have also influenced HTML editors such as FrontPage.

XHTML (extensible hyper-text mark-up language). The latest version of HTML, providing integration with XML and a highly standardised format for compatibility with web browsers. See also W3C, HTML.

XML (extensible mark-up language). A script used to provide semantic and descriptive information within a web context. XML is used alongside traditional web content, VLEs and other systems to enhance content management and searching functionality. See also Metadata, RSS, W3C.

Zip archive. A file compression format allowing for temporary reduced file size. Zip applications such as WinZip (*http://www.winzip.com*) are typically used to compress files within a folder unit called a zip file (ending in .zip). A zip file or 'archive' may be expanded later using a zip application to access files. The Windows XP operating system provides seamless creation and access for zip archives, removing the necessity for additional 'zip' software.

Bibliography

Berners-Lee, T. (2004) *Homepage*. February: *http://www.w3.org/People/ Berners-Lee*.

British Council (2004) *Vision 2020: Forecasting International Student Mobility*. April: *http://www.britishcouncil.org*.

Brockman, J. (2003) 'Quality management and benchmarking: background', in J. Brockman, (ed.), *Quality Management and Benchmarking in the Information Sector*. London: Bowker Saur, pp. 5–6.

Catherall, P. (2000) *Resource Description and Control on the World Wide Web*, MA Dissertation, Liverpool John Moores University, p. 35.

Centre for Educational Technology Interoperability Standards (2004) *Standards Compliant Products Directory*. April: *http://www.cetis.ac .uk/directory/index_html?start=0*.

Charter Mark (2004) *Assessment Criteria*. April: *http://www .chartermark.gov.uk*.

City University, London (2003) *Return to SENDA? Implementing Accessibility for Disabled Students in UK Further and Higher Education*. April: *http://www.saradunn.net/VLEreport/index.html*.

Coffield, F. and Williamson, B. (1997) 'The challenges facing higher education', in F. Coffield and B. Williamson (eds), *Repositioning Higher Education*, Buckingham: Open University Press, p. 8.

Copyright Licensing Agency (2004a) *CLA Digitisation Licensing Scheme*. February: *http://www.cla.co.uk/have_licence/he/he_digitisation.html*.

Copyright Licensing Agency (2004b) *Consultation with UUK/SCOP HEIs – Scanning Rights in CLA Licence: Report of Meeting held on 14 Jan 2004 at Biochemical Society, London*. April: *http://www.pls .org.uk/publisher/HE_consultation_meeting_14Jan_report.htm*.

Department for Education and Employment (1998) *The Learning Age*. March: *http://www.lifelonglearning.co.uk/greenpaper*.

Disability Rights Commission (2004a) *Code of Practice – Rights of Access Goods, Facilities, Services and Premises*. April: *http://www .drc-gb.org/open4all/law/code.asp*.

Disability Rights Commission (2004b) *The Web: Access and Inclusion for Disabled People – A Formal Investigation Conducted by the Disability Rights Commission.* April: *http://www.drc-gb.org/publicationsandreports/report.asp.*

E-Government and Public Sector IT News (2004) *Latest UK Web Access and Usage Patterns from National Statistics: Dec 2003.* May: *http://www.publictechnology.net/modules.php?op=modload&name=News&file=article&sid=380.*

Erskine, J. (2003) *Learning and Teaching Support Network, 'Resource Guide in Virtual Learning Environments (VLEs)'.* February: *http://www.hlst.ltsn.ac.uk/projects/Specialists/erskine.pdf.*

Friesen, N. (2004) *Three Objections to Learning Objects.* February: *http://phenom.educ.ualberta.ca/~nfriesen.*

Good, M. (2001) 'On the way to online pedagogy', in J. Stephenson (ed.), *Teaching & Learning Online: Pedagogies for New Technologies.* London: Kogan Page, p. 169.

Great Britain, Home Office (1993) *Data Protection Act.* London: HMSO.

Great Britain, Home Office (1993) *Welsh Language Act.* London: HMSO.

Great Britain, Home Office (1995) *Disability Discrimination Act.* London: HMSO.

Great Britain, Home Office (1998) *Copyright, Designs and Patents Act.* London: HMSO.

Great Britain, Home Office (2001) *Special Educational Needs and Disability Act.* London: HMSO.

Great Britain, Home Office (2003) *21st Century Skills: Realising Our Potential.* London: HMSO.

Great Britain, Home Office (2003) *Copyright (Visually Impaired Persons) Act.* London: HMSO.

Great Britain, Home Office (2003) *The Future of Higher Education.* London: HMSO.

Higher Education Statistics Agency (2003) *Press Release: Enrolments Rise by 4.3% First 2002/03 Student Enrolment Data Released.* February: *http://www.hesa.ac.uk/press/pr71/pr71.htm.*

HMSO DDA website (2004) *Disability Discrimination Act 1995.* February: *http://www.disability.gov.uk/dda.*

HMSO website (2004) February: *http://www.hmso.gov.uk.*

Information Commissioner's Office (2004) *Disability Discrimination Act Guidance.* April: *http://www.informationcommissioner.gov.uk/eventual.aspx?id=87.*

Jolliffe, A. et al. (2001) *The Online Learning Handbook.* London: Kogan Page, p. 3.

Moore, K. and Aspen, L. (2004) 'Coping, adapting, evolving: the student experience of e-learning', *Update*, 3, 22–4.

National Committee of Inquiry into Higher Education (1997) *The Dearing Report*. March: *http://www.leeds.ac.uk/educol/ncihe*.

National Learning Network (2004) *Paving the Way to Excellence in E-Learning*. April: *http://www.nln.ac.uk/materials/downloads/pdf/paving_the_way.pdf*.

Naughton, J. (1999) *A Brief History of the Future: The Origins of the Internet*. London: Phoenix, pp. 235–48

Office of National Statistics (2003a) *Education, Earnings and Productivity: Recent UK Evidence: Using Recent Labour Force Survey Datasets, the Theory that Education Raises Productivity is Tested*. April: *http://www.statistics.gov.uk/cci/article.asp?id=647*.

Office of National Statistics (2003b) *Student Enrolments on Higher Education Courses at Publicly Funded Higher Education Institutions in the United Kingdom*. April: *http://www.statistics.gov.uk/STATBASE/Product.asp?vlnk=1888*.

Office of National Statistics (2003c) *Student Enrolments on Higher Education Courses at Publicly Funded Higher Education Institutions in the United Kingdom for the Academic Year 2001/2002*. April: *http://www.hesa.ac.uk/Press/sfr56/sfr56.htm*.

Office of National Statistics (2003d) *Yearn to Learn – Higher Education Enrolments Rise 4.3%*. April: *http://www.statistics.gov.uk/cci/nugget.asp?id=9*.

Quality Assurance Agency for Higher Education (2004) *Code of Practice for the Assurance of Academic Quality and Standards in Higher Education*. *http://www.qaa.ac.uk/public/COP/codesofpractice.htm*.

Royal National Institute for the Blind (2004) *Summary: Statistics on Sight Problems in the United Kingdom and Worldwide*. April: *http://www.rnib.org/xpedio/groups/public/documents/PublicWebsite/public_researchstats.hcsp#P1_229*.

Universities and Colleges Information Systems Association (2001) *Management and Implementation of Virtual Learning Environments: A UCISA Funded Survey*. March: *http://www.ucisa.ac.uk/groups/tlig/vle*.

Universities and Colleges Information Systems Association (2003) *VLE Surveys – A Longitudinal Perspective Between March 2001 and March 2003 for Higher Education in the United Kingdom*. March: *http://www.ucisa.ac.uk/groups/tlig/vle*.

World Wide Web Consortium (2004) *Browser Statistics: What is the Trend in Browser Usage, Operating Systems and Screen Resolution?* February: *http://www.w3schools.com/browsers/browsers_stats.asp*

World Wide Web Consortium (2004b) *W3C WAI Statement on DRC Report 2004.* May: *http://www.w3.org/2004/04/wai-drc-statement .html.*

Index

Terms used very often throughout this text such as PC, World Wide Web have not been included in this index. Additional information on terms (including the above) may be found in the Glossary. *Note*: The description 'government paper' indicates both government legislation at any stage or reports derived from government departments or other government organs.